# Thai
## phrasebook

**Consultant**
เรียบเรียง โดย Tasneeya Sae-Mak

First published 2007
Copyright © HarperCollins Publishers
Reprint 10 9 8 7 6 5 4 3 2 1 0
Typeset by Davidson Pre-Press, Glasgow
Printed in Malaysia by Imago

www.collins.co.uk

ISBN 13 978-0-00-724684-7
ISBN 10 0-00-724684-6

## Using your phrasebook

Your *Collins Gem Phrasebook* is designed to help you locate the exact phrase you need, when you need it, whether on holiday or for business. If you want to adapt the phrases, you can easily see where to substitute your own words using the dictionary section, and the clear, full-colour layout gives you direct access to the different topics.

### The Gem Phrasebook includes:

- Over 70 topics arranged thematically. Each phrase is accompanied by a simple pronunciation guide which eliminates any problems pronouncing foreign words.

- A top ten tips section to safeguard against any cultural faux pas, giving essential dos and don'ts for situations involving local customs or etiquette.

- Practical hints to make your stay trouble free, showing you where to go and what to do when dealing with everyday matters such as travel or hotels and offering valuable tourist information.

- Face to face sections so that you understand what is being said to you. These example mini-dialogues give you a good idea of what to expect from a real conversation.

- Common announcements and messages you may hear, ensuring that you never miss the important information you need to know when out and about.

- A clearly laid-out dictionary means you will never be stuck for words.

- A basic grammar section which will enable you to build on your phrases.

- A list of public holidays to avoid being caught out by unexpected opening and closing hours, and to make sure you don't miss the celebrations!

It's worth spending time before you embark on your travels just looking through the topics to see what is covered and becoming familiar with what might be said to you.

Whatever the situation, your *Gem Phrasebook* is sure to help!

# Contents

# Pronouncing Thai

Thai is a tonal language, which means that it needs to be pronounced in the correct tone. Otherwise miscommunication may occur. There are five tones in the Thai language:

## Mid Tone

This is spoken in an ordinary tone of voice without any inflection. It sounds like the tone used in ordinary English conversation. There is no symbol to represent this tone.

| มา | maa | to come |
|------|------|---------|
| ดี | dii | good |
| ใจ | jai | heart |
| ไกล | glai | far |

## Low Tone

This is a level of tone with no inflection. However, it sounds lower in pitch than the mid tone. The symbol used in this phrasebook is ` .

| หนึ่ง | nùng | one |
|-------|------|-----|
| จะ | jà | will |
| ใส่ | sài | to wear |
| ข่าว | kàao | news |

## The Falling Tone

A pronounced, emphasized tone with a falling inflection. It is similar to the tone used in English to denote emphasis. The symbol used in this phrasebook is ^.

| ไม่ | mâi | no, not |
|-----|-----|---------|
| ข้าว | kâao | rice |
| ใช่ | châi | correct |
| นี่ | nîi | this |

## High Tone

This level of tone is above the level of normal tone. It is pronounced in the same way as asking a question in the English language. The symbol used in this phrasebook is ´.

| ม้า | máa | horse |
| วัด | wát | temple |
| รัก | rák | to love |
| รู้ | rúu | to know |

## Rising Tone

This level of tone is similar to the tone used in English to denote surprise. The symbol used in this phrasebook is ˇ.

| หมา | mǎa | dog |
| ใหม | mǎi | silk |
| ขาว | kǎao | white |
| หนังสือ | nǎngsǔu | book |

# Vowels

• • • • • • • • • • • • • • • • • • • • • • • • • • • • • • •

There are two types of vowel: short and long. Short vowels are cut off at the end. Long vowels are drawn out. A long vowel sound is represented by a double letter or a combination of two letters. A short vowel sound is represented by a single letter or a single letter followed by a colon.

## Short and Long vowels

| | | |
|---|---|---|
| **a** | as in | **a**way |
| **aa** | as in | f**a**ther |
| **i** | as in | t**i**p |
| **ii** | as in | b**ee** |
| **u** | as in | g**oo**d |
| **uu** | as in | r**u**le |
| **e** | as in | g**e**t |
| **ee** | as in | p**a**le |
| **o** | as in | b**oa**t |
| **oo** | as in | g**o** |
| **o** | as in | **aw**kward |
| **o** | as in | f**o**r |
| **a:** | as in | h**a**zard |
| **ae** | as **a** in | h**a**ng |
| **u:** | as **e** in | th**e** |
| **ur** | as **u** in | b**ur**n |

# Consonants

The Thai language has 44 consonants and 32 vowel characters. However, there are actually only 20 consonant sounds. In the following list are the consonants that are pronounced in the same way as in English.

| | |
|---|---|
| ก | = **g** as in **g**ood |
| ข ค ฆ | = **k** as in **k**ing |
| จ | = **j** as in **J**anuary |
| ซ ส, ษ, ศ | = **s** as in **s**eek |
| ด, ฎ | = **d** as in **d**oor |
| บ | = **b** as in **b**aby |
| ม | = **m** as in **m**other |
| น ณ | = **n** as in **n**oun |
| ล ฬ | = **l** as in **l**ove |
| ร | = **r** as in **r**oll |
| ว | = **w** as in **w**oman |
| ท ธ | = **t** as in **t**ime |
| ย, ญ | = **y** as in **y**ou |
| ฟ | = **f** as in **f**un |
| ห ฮ | = **h** as in **h**oney |

The following are a few sounds that are difficult to pronounce.

ฎ ต = **dt** as in s**t**op
ป = **bp** as in s**p**ain
ช ฌ ฉ = **ch** as in **ch**ange
ง = **ng** as in ri**ng**ing

The '**dt**' tone is the sound between '**d**' and '**t**'. Similarly, the '**bp**' tone is the sound between '**b**' and '**p**'. Thai people often do not differentiate between the sounds '**r**' and '**l**': these two sounds are usually pronouced in the same tone. The '**ng**' sound in English normally occurs at the end of words. Unlike in English, '**ng**' is often used at the beginning of Thai words.

# Top ten tips

1 Thailand is a Buddhist country. You should dress appropriately when visiting a Buddhist temple. Slippers, shorts, miniskirts and tank tops are not permitted, and shoes should be removed before entering.

2 Thai people hold their King and Queen in great reverence. The national anthem is played twice a day (at 8.00 am and again at 6.00 pm), and also before a film at the cinema. Everyone shows their respect by standing while the anthem is playing, and you will be expected to do the same.

3 It is polite to call Thai people by their first name and add the word **Khun** before it. The word **Khun** can be used for both men and women. It is not used for children.

4 It is normal for people to stand or sit very close to each other when talking, which may be closer than you're used to. Pulling away from your counterpart may be regarded as unfriendly.

5 Public shows of intimacy between men and women are not approved of.

6 Never touch a person's head. Thai people believe that the head is the noblest part of the body.

7 Never use your feet to point things out or to touch any part of another person's body. That is considered very rude.

8 You will be expected to take your shoes off when you enter a Thai house.

9 If you are picking up food with your hands, use your right hand.

10 Women are not allowed to touch a Buddhist monk.

# Talking to people

## Hello/goodbye, yes/no

It is easy to remember how to say hello, good morning, good afternoon and good evening in Thai as the language uses the words สวัสดีครับ/ค่ะ sà-wad-dii krab/ka for any occasion except goodnight.

| | |
|---|---|
| Goodbye | ลานะครับ/ค่ะ |
| | laa na krab/ká |
| Farewell | ลาก่อนครับ/ค่ะ |
| | la kòrn krab/ká |
| See you again | พบกันใหม่ครับ/ค่ะ |
| | pob kan mài krab/ká |
| See you tomorrow | พบกันพรุ่งนี้ |
| | pob-kan-prûng níi |
| Yes | ใช่ครับ/ค่ะ |
| | châi krab/ká |
| No | ไม่ใช่ครับ/ค่ะ |
| | mâi châi krab/ká |

| Please | กรุณา, โปรด |
|---|---|
| | ga-ru-naa, pròot |
| Thank you | ขอบคุณครับ/ค่ะ |
| | kòrb kun-krab/ká |
| Thanks | ขอบใจ |
| | korb-jai |
| Sorry! | ขอโทษครับ/ค่ะ |
| | kör tôot krab/ká! |
| Excuse me! | ประทานโทษครับ/ค่ะ |
| | bpra-taan- tôot krab/ká! |
| I don't understand | ผม/ดิฉันไม่เข้าใจ |
| | pöm/di-chan mâi kâo-jai |
| I cannot speak Thai | ผม/ |
| | ดิฉัน พูดภาษาไทยไม่ได้ |
| | pöm/di-chanpûud paa-säa thai mâi dâi |

# Key phrases

• • • • • • • • • • • • • • • • • • • • • • • • • • • •

| Where is...? | ที่ไหน |
|---|---|
| | tîi näi...? |

| Where is the nearest bank? | ธนาคารที่ใกล้ที่สุดอยู่ที่ไหน |
| | ta-naa-kaan tîi glâi tîi sut yùu tîi näi? |
| Where is the toilet? | ห้องสุขาอยู่ที่ไหน |
| | hô:ng su-käa yùu tîi näi? |
| How...? | เท่าไหร่ |
| | tâo-rài? |
| How much does it cost? | อันนี้เท่าไหร่ครับ/คะ |
| | an níi tâo-rài krab/ká? |
| Is it included...? | มันรวมกับ... |
| | man ruam kàb...? |
| When is/are...? | เมื่อไหร่ |
| | mûa-rài...? |
| When is breakfast? | อาหารเช้าเสริฟตอนกี่โมง |
| | aa-häan cháao surp dtorn gìi moong? |
| When are we going? | เราจะไปเมื่อไหร่ |
| | rao ja bpai mûa-rài? |
| What time is it? | กี่โมงแล้ว |
| | gìi moong láew? |
| At what time...? | ตอนกี่โมง |
| | dtorn gìi moong? |

| What is it? | นี่คืออะไร |
| | nîi kuu a-rai? |
| Which one? | อันไหน |
| | an-näi? |
| Why? | ทำไม |
| | tam mai? |
| Please leave! | กรุณาออกไป |
| | ga-ru-naa òrk bpai! |
| Do you have...? | คุณมี |
| | khun mii ... mái? |
| I would like... | ผม/ดิฉัน ต้องการ... |
| | pöm dtô:ng gaan... |
| I would like a bottle of beer | ผมต้องการเบียร์หนึ่งขวด |
| | pöm dtô:ng gaan beer nùng kùat |
| Can I...? | ขอผม/ดิฉัน ... ได้ไหม |
| | kör pöm/di-chan ... dâai mái? |
| Can I use your phone? | ขอผมใช้โทรศัพท์ได้ไหม |
| | kör pöm chái too-rá-sàp dâai mái? |
| Can I smoke? | ขอผมสูบบุหรี่ได้ไหม |
| | kör pöm sùub burìi dâai mái? |
| There is/are... | ที่นี่มี... |
| | tîi nîi mii... |
| There isn't... | ที่นี่ไม่มี... |
| | tîi nîi mâi mii... |

18

# Signs and notices

| | | |
|---|---|---|
| เปิด | bpùrt | open |
| ปิด | bpìd | closed |
| สุภาพสตรี | sù-pâap-sà-dtrii | Ladies |
| สุภาพบุรุษ | sù-pâap-bu-rut | Gentlemen |
| บริการตนเอง | bo:-ri-gaan-dtua-eeng | self-service |
| ผลัก | plàk | push |
| ดึง | dung | pull |
| ที่จ่ายเงิน | tîi jàai ngurn | cash desk |
| น้ำดื่ม | náam dùum | drinking water |
| ห้องน้ำ/สุขา | hô:ng-náam/su-käa | toilets |
| ว่าง | wâang | vacant |
| ไม่ว่าง | mâi wâang | engaged |
| ห้องฉุกเฉิน | hô:ng chùk chürn | emergency room |

| ปฐมพยาบาล | bpà-tŏm pa-yaa-baan | first aid |
|---|---|---|
| เต็ม | dtem | full |
| หยุด | yùt | stop |
| ปิดซ่อม | bpìd sô:m | out of order |
| ให้เช่า | hâi châo | for rent |
| ขาย | käai | for sale |
| ลดราคา | lót raa-kaa | sales |
| ใต้ถุน | dtâi tün | basement |
| ชั้นล่าง | chán lâang | ground floor |
| ทางเข้า | taang kâo | entrance |
| ที่ขายตั๋ว | tîi käai dtüa | ticket office |
| สถานีตำรวจ | sa-täa-nii dtam-rùat | police station |
| ของหาย | kö:ng häai | lost property |
| ขาออก | käa-òrk | departures |
| ขาเข้า | käa-kâo | arrivals |
| ห้าม | hâam | prohibited |

| | | |
|---|---|---|
| กระเป๋าเดิน ทางที่ถูกลืม | grà-bpǎo-durn- taang tîi tùuk luum | left luggage |
| ส่วนบุคคล | sùan buk-kol | private |
| ร้อน | rórn | hot |
| หนาว/เย็น | nǎao/yen | cold |
| อันตราย | an-dta-raai | danger |
| ห้ามสูบบุหรี่ | hâam sùub-bu-rìi | no smoking |
| กรุณาอย่าจับ | ka-ru-naa yàa jàb | do not touch |
| ทางออก | taang-òrk | exit |
| ห้องเปลี่ยน เสื้อผ้า | hô:ng bplìan sûa-pâa | changing room |
| ห้องน้ำ | hô:ng náam | bathroom |
| ระวัง | ra-wang | caution |
| ข้อมูล | kôr-moon | information |
| สอบถาม | sòrb-thǎam | enquiries |

# Polite expressions

. . . . . . . . . . . . . . . . . . . . . . . . . . . . .

Thailand is a land of smiles and Thai people are kind and friendly. One easy way to add politeness to a sentence is to add the word ครับ krab (for men/boys) or คะ ká (for women/girls) at the end of the sentence. For example:

| How are you? | สบายดีไหมครับ |
| (to be said by a man/boy) | sà baai dii mái krab? |
| (to be said by a woman/girl) | สบายดีไหมคะ |
| | sà baai dii mái ká? |

Traditionally, Thai people greet each other with the ไหว้ wai action, which involves pressing the palms together in front of the chest and bowing the head a little, and saying 'sà-wàd-dii krab/ká.'

| How do you do? | สบายดีไหมครับ/คะ |
| | sà baai dii mái krab/ká? |
| I am fine | ผม/ดิฉัน สบายดี |
| | pöm/di-chan sà baai dii |
| Thank you | ขอบคุณ |
| | kòrb kun |

| | |
|---|---|
| My name is... | ผม/ดิฉัน ชื่อ...<br>pöm/di-chan chûu... |
| Welcome! | ยินดีต้อนรับ<br>yindii dtôrn rab |
| Yes, Sir | ครับ/ค่ะ<br>krab/ká |
| Pardon me/<br>Excuse me | ขอโทษครับ/คะ<br>kör toot krab/ká |
| This is... | นี่คือ...<br>nîi kuu... |
| This is my<br>husband (wife) | นี่คือภรรยา (สามี)<br>ของผม/ดิฉัน<br>nîi kuu panrayaa (säamii) kö:ng<br>pöm/dichan |
| Enjoy your meal! | ทานอาหารให้อร่อย<br>นะครับ/คะ<br>taan aa-häan hâi aròy na krab/ká! |
| Pleased to meet<br>you | ยินดีที่ได้รู้จักครับ/ค่ะ<br>yin dii tîi dâai rúu-jàk krab/ká |
| The meal was<br>delicious | อาหารอร่อยมากครับ/ค่ะ<br>aa-häan aròy mâak krab/ká |
| Thank you very<br>much | ขอบคุณมากครับ/ค่ะ<br>kòrb kun mâak krab/ká |

| Have a good trip! | เดินทางให้สนุกครับ/ค่ะ |
| | durn taang hâi sa-nuk krab/ká! |
| Enjoy your holiday! | เที่ยวให้สนุกนะครับ/ค่ะ |
| | tieew hâi sanuk na krab/ká! |

# Celebrations

· · · · · · · · · · · · · · · · · · · · · · · · ·

| Happy birthday! | สุขสันต์วันเกิด |
| | sùk-sän wan gùrt! |
| Congratulations! | ยินดีด้วยครับ/ค่ะ |
| | yin dii dôay krab/ká! |
| Cheers! (when you raise your glass) | ไชโย |
| | chai-yo! |
| Happy New Year! | สวัสดีปีใหม่ |
| | sa-wad-dii bpii mài! |

# Making friends

· · · · · · · · · · · · · · · · · · · · · · · · ·

| Hello my name is... | สวัสดีครับ/ค่ะ ผม/ดิฉัน ชื่อ... |
| | sa-wad-dii krab/ká pöm/ di-chan chûu... |

24    > **Public holidays** (p 163)

| | |
|---|---|
| What is your name? | คุณชื่ออะไรครับ/คะ<br>khun chûu a-rai krab/ka? |
| Where are you from? | คุณมาจากประเทศอะไร<br>khun maa jàak bpra têet a-rai? |
| I am from England | ผม/ดิฉัน มาจากประเทศ<br>อังกฤษ<br>pŏm/di-chan maa jàak bpra têet<br>ang-grìt |
| Nice to meet you | ยินดีที่ได้รู้จักคุณ<br>yindii tîi dâai rúu jàk |
| How old are you? | คุณอายุเท่าไหร่<br>khun aa-yú tâo-rài? |
| I'm ... years old | ผม/ดิฉัน อายุ ... ปี<br>pŏm/di-chan aa-yú ... bpii |
| Where do you live? | คุณอยู่ที่ไหน<br>khun yùu tîi näi? |
| I live in London | ผม/ดิฉัน อยู่ในลอนดอน<br>pŏm/di-chan yùu tîi london |
| Are you married? | คุณแต่งงานแล้วหรือยัง<br>khun dtàeng-ngaan láew rʉ̌u yang? |
| Do you have any children? | คุณมีลูกหรือยัง<br>khun mii lûuk rʉ̌u yang? |
| I have children | ผม/ดิฉัน มีลูกแล้ว<br>pŏm/di-chan mii lûuk láew |

| | |
|---|---|
| I don't have children | ผม / ดิฉัน ไม่มีลูก |
| | pöm/di-chan mâi mii lûuk |
| I have a boyfriend/ girlfriend | ผม / ดิฉัน มีแฟนแล้ว |
| | pöm/di-chan mii faen láew |
| I'm single | ผม / ดิฉัน เป็นโสด |
| | pöm/di-chan bpen sòot |
| I'm married | ผม / ดิฉัน แต่งงานแล้ว |
| | pöm/di-chan dtàeng-ngaan láew |
| I'm divorced | ผม / ดิฉัน เป็นหม้าย |
| | pöm/di-chan bpen mâai |

## Work

. . . . . . . . . . . . . . . . . . . . . . . . . . . . . . . .

| | |
|---|---|
| What is your job? | คุณทำงานอะไร |
| | khun tam-ngaan a-rai? |
| Do you enjoy it? | คุณชอบงานของคุณไหม |
| | khun chôrb ngaan kö:ng khun mái? |
| I'm a doctor | ผม / ดิฉัน เป็นหมอ |
| | pöm/di-chan bpen mör |
| I'm a teacher | ผม / ดิฉัน เป็นครู |
| | pöm/di-chan bpen kruu |

26

> **Leisure/beach** (p 79) > **Sport** (p 85)

| I'm a nurse | ผม/ดิฉัน เป็น บุรุษพยาบาล/พยาบาล |
| | pöm/di-chan bpen bu-rut pa-yaa-baan/pa-yaa-baan |
| I work in a shop | ผม/ดิฉัน ทำงานในร้านค้า |
| | pöm/di-chan tam-ngaan nai ráan káa |
| I work in a factory | ผม/ดิฉัน ทำงานในโรงงาน |
| | pöm/di-chan tam-ngaan nai roong-ngaan |
| I work in a bank | ผม/ดิฉัน ทำงานในธนาคาร |
| | pöm/di-chan tam-ngaan nai ta-naa-kaan |
| I work from home | ผม/ดิฉัน ทำงานที่บ้าน |
| | pöm/di-chan tam-ngaan tîi bâan |

Work

> **Making friends** (p 24)

# Weather

| สดใส  sòd-sǎi | clear |
|---|---|
| ฝนตก  fǒn-dtòk | rainy |
| หนาว  nǎao | cold |
| ร้อน  rórn | hot |
| ฟ้าใส  fáa sǎi | sunny |
| ลมแรง  lom-raeng | windy |
| พยากรณ์อากาศ  pa-yaa-korn aa-gàat | weather forecast |

It's sunny        แดดออก
                  dàed òrk

It's raining      ฝนกำลังตก
                  fǒn gamlang dtòk

It's windy        ลมแรงทีเดียว
                  lom-raeng tii-diao

It's very hot     ร้อนมากมาก
                  rórn mâak mâak

| | |
|---|---|
| What is the temperature? | อุณหภูมิเท่าไหร่<br>un-hà-puum tâo rài? |
| What is the weather forecast for tomorrow? | พรุ่งนี้อากาศจะเป็นอย่างไร<br>prûng níi aa-gàat ja bpen yaang-rài? |
| Does it get cool at night? | ตอนกลางคืนอากาศหนาวไหม<br>dtorn glaang-kuun aa-gàat năao mái? |
| Will there be a storm? | จะมีพายุไหม<br>ja mii paa-yu mái? |
| What beautiful weather! | อากาศดีจริงจริง<br>aa-gàat dii jing jing! |
| What awful weather! | อากาศไม่ดี<br>aa-gàat mâi dii! |

# Getting around

## Asking the way

| | |
|---|---|
| ซ้าย   sáai | left |
| ขวา   kwäa | right |
| ตรงไป   dtrong bpai | straight on |
| ตรงข้ามกับ<br>dtrong kâam kàp | opposite |
| ติดกับ   dtìd kàp | next to |
| ไฟจราจร<br>fai ja-raa-jorn | traffic lights |
| ตรงหัวมุม<br>dtrong hüa mum | at the corner |

**FACE TO FACE**

**A** ขอโทษครับ/ค่ะ
   ที่ทำการไปรษณีย์อยู่ที่ไหนครับ/คะ
   kör-tôot krab/ka tîi tam-gaanbprai-sa-nii yùu tîi näi
   krab/ka?
   Excuse me. Where is the post office?

**B** เดินตรงไป แล้วเลี้ยวขวา/ซ้าย ตรงหัวมุม
   durn dtrong bpai láew líao kwäa/sái dtrong hüa-mum
   Keep straight on and turn right/left at the corner

**A** ไกลไหมครับ/คะ
   glai mái krab/ká?
   Is it far?

**B** ไม่ไกลครับ/ค่ะ ห่างแค่ 200 เมตร/
   2 นาที
   mâi glai krab/ka hàang kâe so:ng-ro:y met/
   so:ng naa-tii
   No. Only 200 metres/2 minutes away

**A** ขอบคุณครับ/ค่ะ
   kòrb kun - krab/ká
   Thank you

**B** ไม่เป็นไรครับ/ค่ะ
   mâi bpen rai krab/ka
   You are welcome

Asking the way

31

| | |
|---|---|
| Where is...? | ...อยู่ไหน |
| | ...yùu näi? |
| Where is the museum? | พิพิธภัณฑ์อยู่ไหน |
| | pi-pit-ta-pan yùu näi? |
| How do I get...? | ผม/ดิฉัน จะไป ... ได้อย่างไร |
| | pöm/di-chan ja bpai ... dâai yàang rai? |
| How do I get to the museum? | ผม/ดิฉัน จะไปพิพิธภัณฑ์ ได้อย่างไร |
| | pöm/di-chan ja bpai pi-pit-ta-pan dâi yàang rai? |
| to the coach station | ไปท่ารถขนส่ง |
| | bpai tâa rót kön sòng |
| to the beach | ไปที่ชายหาด |
| | bpai tîi chaai-hàat |
| to my hotel | ไปที่โรงแรมของฉัน |
| | bpai tîi roong-raem kö:ng chan |

| | |
|---|---|
| เลี้ยวซ้าย<br>líao sáai | Turn left |
| เลี้ยวขวา<br>líao kwäa | Turn right |
| เดินตรงไป<br>durn dtrong bpai | Keep straight on |
| ใกล้ใกล้<br>glâi glâi | Closer to |

# Bus and coach

..........................................

Buses and coaches are the cheapest way to travel in Thailand. Bus services are provided by the government. If you plan to travel around Bangkok by bus, you can get a free copy of the city's maps from the TAT (Tourism Authority of Thailand) counter at the airport. Coach services are operated by both the government and private companies. The private companies charge a little more than the government-run coach service does, but they are faster and more comfortable.

> **Maps and guides** (p 71)

| ท่ารถเมล์ tâa rót meey | bus stop |
| ท่ารถขนส่ง<br>tâa rót kön sòng | coach station |
| ตั๋ว dtüa | ticket |

**FACE TO FACE**

**A** ขอโทษครับ/ค่ะ รถไปเชียงใหม่ออกเวลา 10 โมงคันไหนครับ/คะ

kör-tôot krab/ka rót bpai chiang mai ork wei-laa sìp moong kan näi krab/ka?

Excuse me. Which one is the 10 o'clock Chiang Mai bus?

**B** คันทางซ้าย/ขวา สีน้ำเงินครับ/ค่ะ

kan taang sáai/kwäa sïi náam-ngurn krab/ká

The one on the right/left. The blue bus.

| Where is the coach station? | ท่ารถขนส่งอยู่ที่ไหนครับ/คะ |
| | tâa rót kön sòng yùu näi krab/ká? |
| I am going to... | ผม/ดิฉัน กำลังจะไป... |
| | pöm/dichan kamlang ja bpai... |

| | |
|---|---|
| Is there a bus to...? | มีรถไป ... ไหมครับ/คะ<br>mii rót bpai ... mái krab/ká? |
| Does it go to...? | มันไปถึง ... ไหมครับ/ค่ะ<br>man bpai tüng ... mái krab/ká? |
| It goes to... | มันไปถึง...<br>man bpai tüng... |
| the airport | ท่าอากาศยาน<br>bpai tâa aa-gàat-sa-yaan |
| the beach | ชายหาด<br>bpai chaai-hàat |
| the shopping centre | ศูนย์การค้า<br>bpai süun gaan káa |
| 1 ticket | ตั๋วหนึ่งใบ<br>dtüa nùng bai |
| 2 tickets | ตั๋วสองใบ<br>dtüa sö:ng bai |
| 3 tickets | ตั๋วสามใบ<br>dtüa säam bai |
| When is the next bus? | รถเที่ยวหน้ากี่โมงครับ/<br>คะ<br>rót tîew nâa kìi moong krab/ká? |

| | |
|---|---|
| **YOU MAY HEAR...** | |
| ไม่มีรถบริการเหลือ แลวครับ/คะ <br> mâi mii rót bo:-ri- gaan láew krab/ká | There is no bus |
| คุณต้องไปรถแท็กซี่ <br> khun tô:ng bpai rót tá:k-sîi | You must take a taxi |
| ตั๋วขายหมดแล้วครับ/ค่ะ <br> dtŭa kăi mòt láew krab/ká | The tickets are sold out |

# Metro/Sky train

• • • • • • • • • • • • • • • • • • • • • • • • • • • • • • • • • • • •

Bangkok is the only city that has metro and sky train services which run from 6 am to 12 pm. Fares range from 14 – 36 baht. Monthly tickets are also available.

| ทางเข้า | taang kâo | entrance |
|---|---|---|
| ทางออก | taang-òrk | way out |

| Where is the nearest metro station? | สถานีรถไฟใต้ดินที่ใกล้ที่ สุดอยู่ที่ไหนครับ/ค่ะ <br> sa-tăa-nii rót fai dtâi din tîi glâi tîi sut yùu tîi näi krab/ká? |
|---|---|

| | |
|---|---|
| How does the ticket machine work? | เครื่องขายตั๋วอัตโนมัติใช้ยังไงครับ/คะ |
| | krûang käi dtüa àt-tà-noo-mát chái yang ngai krab/ká? |
| Do you have a map of the metro? | คุณมีแผนที่ของรถไฟใต้ดินไหมครับ/คะ |
| | khun mii päen-tîi rót fai dtâi din mái krab/ká? |
| I'm going to... | ผมจะไป... |
| | pöm ja bpai... |
| How do I/we get to...? | ผม/พวกเรา จะไป ... ได้อย่างไร |
| | pöm/puag-rao ja bpai ... dâai yang rai? |
| Do I have to change? | ผมต้องเปลี่ยนรถไหม |
| | pöm dtô:ng bplian rót mái? |
| What is the next stop? | ป้ายหน้าอะไรครับ/คะ |
| | bpâi nâa a-rai krab/ká? |
| Excuse me. I'm getting off here | ขอโทษครับ/ค่ะ ผม/ดิฉัน จะลงป้ายนี้ |
| | kör-tôot krab/ká pöm/di-chan ja long bpâi níi |
| Please let me through | ขอทางด้วยครับ/ค่ะ |
| | kör taang dûai krab/ká |

> **Luggage** (p 99)

# Train

• • • • • • • • • • • • • • • • • • • • • • • • • • • • • • • • • • •

Train services are offered throughout the country
and the fares are very reasonable. The train centre
in Bangkok is Hualamphong Station หัวลำโพง
hua-lam-phong.

Getting around

| สถานี sa-täa-nii | station |
|---|---|
| รถไฟ rót fai | train |
| ชานชาลา chaan-chaa-laa | platform |
| ที่นั่ง tîi nâng | seat |
| ตั๋ว dtüa | ticket |
| ที่ขายตั๋ว tîi käai dtüa | booking office |
| ตารางเวลา dtaa-raang wee-laa | timetable |
| เปลี่ยนเส้นทาง bplìan sên taang | connection |

> **Luggage** (p 99)

**A** รถไฟไปส่งขลาเที่ยวหน้ากี่โมงครับ/คะ

rót fai bpai söng-kläa tîao nâa gìi moong krab/ka?

**When is the next train to Song Khla?**

**B** สิบโมง

sìp moong

**At 10 o'clock**

**A** ซื้อตั๋วสามใบ

súu dtŭa säam bai

**3 tickets please**

**B** ตั๋วเที่ยวเดียวหรือไปกลับ

dtŭa tîao diao rüu bpai glàb?

**Single or return?**

**A** ไปกลับ

bpai glàb

**Return, please**

| | |
|---|---|
| Where is the station? | สถานีรถไฟอยู่ไหน |
| | sa-täa-nii rót fai yùu näi? |
| a single | เที่ยวเดียว |
| | tîao diao |

| | |
|---|---|
| 2 singles | เที่ยวเดียวสองใบ |
| | tîao diao sö:ng bai |
| a single to Lum Pang | ตั๋วเที่ยวเดียวหนึ่งใบไป ลำปาง |
| | dtüa tîao diao nùng bai bpai lum-pang |
| 2 singles to Sukothai | ตั๋วเที่ยวเดียวสองใบไป สุโขทัย |
| | dtüa tîao diao sö:ng bai bpai su-köo-tai |
| a return | ตั๋วไปกลับ |
| | dtüa bpai glàb |
| 2 returns | ตั๋วไปกลับสองใบ |
| | dtüa bpai glàb sö:ng bai |
| 1 adult | ผู้ใหญ่หนึ่งคน |
| | pûu yài nùng kon |
| 2 children | เด็กสองคน |
| | dèk sö:ng kon |
| 2 adults | ผู้ใหญ่สองคน |
| | pûu yài sö:ng kon |
| first class | ชั้นหนึ่ง |
| | chán nùng |

| second class | ชั้นสอง |
| | chán sö:ng |
| smoking | สูบบุหรี่ได้ |
| | sùub burii dâai |
| non-smoking | ห้ามสูบบุหรี่ |
| | hâam sùub burii |
| I want to book a seat | ฉันต้องการจองตั๋วหนึ่งใบ |
| | chan tô:ng gaan jorng dtüa nùng bai |
| Which platform? | ชานชาลาไหน |
| | chaan-chaa-laa näi? |
| When does it get to Nakhon Pathom? | จะไปถึงนครปฐมกี่โมง |
| | ja bpai tüng na-korn-bpa-töm gìi moong? |
| When does it leave? | มันจะออกตอนกี่โมง |
| | man ja òrk dtorn gìi moong? |
| When does it arrive? | มันไปถึงตอนกี่โมง |
| | man bpai tüng dtorn gìi moong? |
| Is this seat free? | ที่นั่งนี้ว่างไหม |
| | tîi nâng níi wâang mái? |
| Excuse me! | ขอโทษ |
| | kör-tôot! |

# Taxi

Taxi services in Bangkok are very convenient, and you can hire one by either hailing it from the street or telephoning the service provider. The telephones used to call taxi services are installed at most of the bus stops in Bangkok.

| | |
|---|---|
| Where can I get a taxi? | ฉันจะเรียกแท็กซี่ได้ที่ไหน<br>chan ja rîak tá:k-sîi dâai tîi näi? |
| I want to go to... | ผม/ดิฉัน ต้องการไปที่...<br>pöm/di-chan tô:ng gaan bpai tîi... |
| How much is it? | เท่าไหร่<br>tâo rài? |
| To the airport, please | ไปสนามบิน<br>bpai sà-näam-bin |
| To the beach, please | ไปชายหาด<br>bpai chaai-hàat |
| Please stop here | จอดตรงนี้<br>jòrt dtrong níi |
| Please wait | ช่วยรอตรงนี้<br>chûai ror dtrong níi |

 > **Luggage** (p 99)

| It's too expensive | มันแพงมาก |
| | man paeng mâak |
| I haven't got any change | ฉันไม่มีเศษสตางค์ |
| | chan mâi mii sèet-sa-taang |
| Keep the change | ไม่ต้องคืนตังทอน |
| | mâi dtô:ng kuun dtang torn |

# Boat

In Bangkok there are several types of boat services on the Chao Phraya River. The motorboat service runs between Wat Ratchasingkhon and Nonthaburi province. The Chao Phraya Tourist boat stops at major places in Bangkok, such as the Grand Palace, Wat Pho and Chinatown. The Long-tail Boat offers a Chao Phraya River tour for small private groups.

| ที่ขายตั๋ว  tîi käai dtüa | ticket office |
|---|---|
| ตารางเวลา dtaa-raang wee-laa | timetable |
| ขาเข้า  käa-kâo | arrival |
| ขาออก  käa-òrk | departure |

| When is the next boat? | เรือเที่ยวหน้ามาเมื่อใหร่<br>rua tîao nâa maa mûa rai? |
| When is the last boat? | เรือเที่ยวสุดท้ายตอนกี่โมง<br>rua tîao sut tái dtorn gìi moong? |
| We want to go to... | เราต้องการจะไป...<br>rao dtô:ng gaan ja bpai... |
| Is there a timetable? | ตารางเวลาเรืออยู่ที่ใหน<br>dtaa-raang wee-laa rua yùu tîi näi? |
| When does the boat leave? | เรือจะออกตอนกี่โมง<br>rua ja òrk dtorn gìi moong? |
| How long does it take? | ใช้เวลานานเท่าใหร่<br>chái wee-laa naan tâo rài? |

# Air travel

· · · · · · · · · · · · · · · · · · · · · · · · · · · · · · ·

| สนามบิน sà-näam-bin | airport |
| ประตู bpra-dtuu | gate |
| ขาเข้า käa-kâo | arrivals |
| ขาออก käa-òrk | departures |
| เที่ยวบิน tîao bin | flight |

44

| ภายในประเทศ<br>paai-nai bpra-têet | domestic |
| นานาชาติ<br>naa-naa- châat | international |
| ข้อมูล  kôr-muun | information |

| To the airport, please | ไปสนามบิน<br>bpai sà-näam-bin |
| My flight is at ... o'clock | เครื่องผม /<br> ดิฉัน ออกตอน ... โมง<br>krûang pöm/di-chan òrk<br> dtorn ... moong |
| How much is it to the airport? | ไปสนามบินเท่าไหร่<br>bpai sà-näam-bin tâo rài? |
| How much is it to the town centre? | ไปใจกลางเมืองเท่าไหร่<br>bpai jai glaang muang tâo rài? |
| When will the flight leave? | เครื่องจะออกเมื่อไหร่<br>krûang ja òrk mûa rai? |

Air travel

**YOU MAY HEAR...**

| ไปที่ประตูเบอร์...<br>bpai tîi bpra dtuu bur... | Go to gate number... |

# Customs control

The import, export, possession or use of drugs is forbidden and penalties for offenders are severe.

| หนังสือเดินทาง<br>näng-süu-durn-taang | passport |
| --- | --- |
| ศุลกากร<br>sün-la-gaa-gorn | customs |
| ของมึนเมา/ ยาสูบ<br>kö:ng mun mao/yaa-sùub | alcohol/ tobacco |

| Do I have to pay duty on this? | อันนี้ฉันต้องเสียภาษีไหม<br>an níi chan dtô:ng sìa paa-síi mài? |
| --- | --- |
| It is my medicine | มันเป็นยาของฉัน<br>man bpen yaa kö:ng chan |
| The children are on this passport | เด็ก ๆ รวมอยู่ในหนังสือ<br>เดินทางเล่มนี้<br>dèk dèk ruam yùu nai näng-süu-<br>durn-taang lêm níi |
| I bought this duty-free | ฉันซื้ออันนี้จากร้านสินค้า<br>ปลอดภาษี<br>chan súu an níi jàak ráan sïn-káa<br>bplòrt paa-síi |

# Driving

## Car hire

Big cities such as Bangkok, Chiang Mai, Pattaya and Phuket have cars and motorcycles for rent. Most of the car rental companies have their offices in medium to large hotels.

| หนังสือประกันภัย näng-süu bpra-gan pai | insurance documents |
| ใบขับขี่   bai-kàp-kìi | driving licence |

| I want to hire a car | ฉันต้องการเช่ารถ chan dtô:ng gaan châo rót |
| with automatic gears | ขอเกียร์ออโตเมติก kör gia or-dtoo-mee-dtik |
| for 1 day | หนึ่งวัน nùng wan |
| for 2 days | สองวัน sö:ng wan |

47

| How much is it? | เท่าไหร่ |
| | tâo rài? |
| Is insurance included? | รวมค่าประกันไหม |
| | ruam kâa bpra-gan mái? |
| Is there a deposit to pay? | ต้องจ่ายเงินมัดจำไหม |
| | dtô:ng jàai ngurn mát-jam mái? |
| Can I pay by credit card? | ฉันใช้เครดิตการ์ดจ่ายได้ไหม |
| | chan chái kree-dit-gáat jàai dâai mái? |
| What petrol does it take? | มันใช้น้ำมันประเภทไหน |
| | man chái náam-man bpra-pêet näi? |

## Driving

. . . . . . . . . . . . . . . . . . . . . . . . . . . .

Driving a car in Bangkok can be difficult; the traffic is bad, especially during the rush hours. For long-distance driving, especially in the southern areas, you should be aware that some of the roads are narrow and you should drive with extra care.

| ระวัง/อันตราย | caution/danger |
| ra-wang/an-dta-raai | |

| หยุด   yùt | stop |
| ทางด่วน   taang dùan | motorway |
| ใจกลางเมือง<br>jai glaang muang | town centre |

| Can I park here? | ฉันจอดตรงนี้ได้ไหม<br>chan jòrt dtrong níi dâai mái? |
| How long can<br>I park for? | ฉันจอดตรงนี้ได้กี่ชั่วโมง<br>chan jòrt dtrong níi dâai gìi<br>chûa-moong? |
| We are driving<br>to... | เราจะขับไปที่...<br>rao ja kàp bpai tîi... |
| Is the road good? | สภาพถนนดีไหม<br>sa-paab tà-nön dii mái? |
| How long will<br>it take? | ใช้เวลากี่ชั่วโมง<br>chái wee-laa gìi chûa-moong? |

Driving

| YOU MAY HEAR... | |
| คุณขับรถเร็วเกินไป<br>khun kàp rót reo gurn bpai | You are driving too fast |
| ขอดูใบขับขี่<br>kör duu bai kàp-kìi | Your driving licence,<br>please |

49

# Petrol

Petrol is widely available at petrol stations, which are found along most roads.

| | |
|---|---|
| น้ำมันเบ็นซิน<br>náam man ben-sin | petrol |
| เบ็นซินไร้สารตะกั่ว<br>ben-sin rái säan ta-gùa | unleaded petrol |
| ดีเซล   dii-sell | diesel |

| | |
|---|---|
| Where is the nearest petrol station? | ปั๊มน้ำมันที่ใกล้ที่สุดอยู่ที่ไหน<br>bpám náam man tîi glâi tîi sut yùu tîi näi? |
| Fill it up, please | เต็มถัง<br>dtem täng |
| unleaded | เบ็นซินไร้สารตะกั่ว<br>ben-sin rái säan ta-gùa |
| diesel | ดีเซล<br>dii-sell |
| Please check the oil | ตรวจน้ำมันด้วย<br>dtrùat náam man dûai |

| Can I pay by credit card? | ฉันใช้เครดิตการ์ดจ่ายได้ไหม |
| | chan chái kree-dit-gáat jàai dâai mái? |

| **YOU MAY HEAR...** | |
|---|---|
| เราไม่มี...<br>rao mâi mii... | We have no... |
| คุณต้องเปลี่ยนน้ำมันเครื่อง/ใส่น้ำ/เติมแอร์<br>khun dtô:ng bplìan náam man krûang/sài náam/dturm air | You need oil/water/air |

# Breakdown

Most of the petrol stations have their own mechanics who are able to help with car problems, should you have any.

| My car has broken down | รถของฉันเสีย |
| | rót kö:ng chan sĭa |

| | |
|---|---|
| Can you help me? | คุณจะช่วยผม/<br>ดิฉัน ได้ไหม<br>khun ja chûai pöm/<br>di-chan dâai mái? |
| I've run out<br>of petrol | รถผม/ดิฉัน น้ำมันหมด<br>rót pöm/di-chan náam man mòd |
| I have a flat tyre | รถผม/ดิฉัน ยางแบน<br>rót pöm/di-chan yaang baen |
| Where is the<br>nearest garage?<br>(repair shop) | อู่ซ่อมรถที่ใกล้ที่สุดอยู่<br>ที่ไหน<br>ùu sô:m rót tîi glâi tîi sut yùu tîi näi? |
| Can you repair it? | คุณจะซ่อมมันได้ไหม<br>khun ja sô:m man dâai mái? |
| How long will<br>it take? | ใช้เวลานานเท่าไหร่<br>chái wee-laa naan tâo rài? |
| How much will<br>it cost? | จะต้องจ่ายเท่าไหร่<br>ja dtô:ng jàai tâo rài? |

# Car parts

• • • • • • • • • • • • • • • • • • • • • • • • • • • • • • • •

| | |
|---|---|
| ...doesn't work | ...เสีย<br>...sïa |

| Where is the repair shop? | อู่ซ่อมรถอยู่ที่ไหน | ùu sô:m rót yùu tîi nǎi? |
|---|---|---|
| accelerator | คันเร่ง | kan rêng |
| alternator | ไดชาร์ต | dai cháat |
| battery | แบ็ตเตอรี่ | ba:t-tur-rii |
| brakes | เบรค | breek |
| choke | โช้ค | chook |
| clutch | คลัทช์ | klatch |
| engine | เครื่องยนต์ | krûang-yon |
| exhaust pipe | ท่อไอเสีย | tôr-ai- sǐa |
| fuse | ฟิวส์ | fiu |
| gears | เกียร์ | giaa |
| handbrake | เบรคมือ | breek-mu |
| headlights | ไฟหน้า | fai-nâa |
| ignition | ระบบจุด ระเบิด | ra-bob- jut-ra- bùrt |
| ignition key | กุญแจ | gun-jae |
| indicator | สัญญาณไฟ | sän-yaan-fai |
| lock | ล็อค | lo:ck |
| radiator | หม้อน้ำ | môr náam |
| reverse gear | เกียร์ถอยหลัง | gia to:y läng |

| | | |
|---|---|---|
| seat belt | เข็มขัดนิรภัย | këm-kat nì-ra-pai |
| spark plug | หัวเทียน | hüa tian |
| steering wheel | พวงมาลัย | puang-maa-lai |
| tyre | ยาง | yaang |
| wheel | ล้อ | lór |
| windscreen | กระจกหน้า | gra-jòk-nâa |
| windscreen wiper | ที่ปัดน้ำฝน | tîi-pat-náam-fön |

## Road signs

Thai speed limits are in kilometres per hour. Tolls are charged on some motorways.

| ห้ามกลับรถ | hâam klàp rót | no U-turn |
|---|---|---|
| ทางเข้า | taang kâo | entrance |
| ทางออก | taang-òrk | exit |
| ทางด่วน | taang dùan | motorway |
| ถนน | tà-nön | road |
| เลี้ยวซ้าย | líao sáai | turn left |
| เลี้ยวขวา | líao kwäa | turn right |

| | | |
|---|---|---|
| เดินรถทางเดียว | durn rót taang diao | one way |
| สุดทางใหญ่ | sut-taang-yài | major road ends |
| ห้ามเข้า | hâam kâo | no entry |
| เหนือ | nŭa | north |
| ใต้ | dtâai | south |
| ตะวันออก | dta-wan- òrk | east |
| ตะวันตก | dta-wan- dtòk | west |
| ทางข้ามถนน | taang kâam tà-nŏn | pedestrian crossing |
| ใจกลางเมือง | jai glaang muang | city centre |
| ลดความเร็ว | lod-kwaam reo | reduce speed |
| ห้ามทำเสียงรบกวน | hâam tam sĭang róp-guan | no sounding of horn |
| หยุด | yùt | stop |
| อันตราย | an-dta-raai | danger |
| โรงพยาบาล | roong-pa-yaa-baan | hospital |
| ห้ามจอด | hâam jòrt | no parking |
| ที่จอด | tîi jòrt | parking |

# Staying somewhere

## Hotel (booking)

Hotels are rated in stars from 1 to 5. Big cities such as Bangkok, Phuket and Chiang Mai also have guesthouses and bed and breakfasts.

| โรงแรม<br>roong-raem | hotel |
|---|---|
| เกสท์เฮาส์/<br>  ห้องเช่าพร้อม<br>  อาหารเช้า<br>guesthouse/hô:ng-châo<br>  pró:m aa-häan cháo | guesthouse/<br>  bed and breakfast |
| ว่าง/ไม่ว่าง<br>wâang/mâi wâang | vacancies/<br>  no vacancies |

**A** เราต้องการจอง ห้องเดี่ยว/ห้องคู่ หนึ่งห้อง
rao dtô:ng gaan jorng hô:ng-dìao/hô:ng-kûu nùng
   hô:ng
We would like to book a single/double room

**B** จองกี่คืน
jo:ng gìi kuun?
For how many nights?

**A** หนึ่งคืน/สองคืน/หนึ่งอาทิตย์
nùng kuun/sö:ng kuun/nùng aa-tít
for one night/two nights/one week

| | |
|---|---|
| Is there a hotel/ guesthouse nearby? | ใกล้ใกล้นี้มีโรงแรมหรือ เกสท์เฮาส์ไหม<br>glâi glâi níi mii roong-raem rüu guesthouse mái? |
| Do you have a room? | มีห้องว่างไหม<br>mii hô:ng wâang mái? |
| I'd like... | ฉันต้องการ...<br>chan dtô:ng gaan... |
| a single room | ห้องเดี่ยว<br>hô:ng dìao |
| a double room | ห้องคู่<br>hô:ng kûu |

57

| a room for 3 people | ห้องสำหรับสามคน |
| | hô:ng säm-ràp säam kon |
| with shower | พร้อมฝักบัว |
| | prórm fàk-bua |
| with bath | พร้อมอ่างอาบน้ำ |
| | prórm àang àap náam |
| How much is it per night? | ต่อคืนราคาเท่าไหร่ |
| | dtòr kuun raa-kaa tâo rài? |
| Is breakfast included? | รวมอาหารเช้าไหม |
| | ruam aa-häan cháao mái? |
| I'll be staying... | ฉันจะอยู่... |
| | chan ja yùu... |
| We'll be staying... | เราจะอยู่... |
| | rao ja yùu... |
| 1 night | หนึ่งคืน |
| | nùng kuun |
| 2 nights | สองคืน |
| | sö:ng kuun |
| 3 nights | สามคืน |
| | säam kuun |
| Is there anywhere else to stay? | มีที่พักที่อื่นอีกบ้างไหม |
| | mii tîi-pák tîi ùun ìik bâang mái? |

| | |
|---|---|
| กรุณาบอกชื่อของคุณ<br>ka-ru-naa bò:k chûu köng khun | Your name, please |
| ขอดูหนังสือเดินทาง<br>kör duu näng-süu-durn-taang | Your passport, please |
| ห้องเต็ม<br>hô:ng dtem | We are full |

# Hotel (desk)

| | |
|---|---|
| I have a reservation | ฉันจองห้องไว้<br>chan jo:ng hô:ng wái |
| My name is... | ฉันชื่อ...<br>chan chûu... |
| Have you a different room? | มีห้องอื่นอีกไหม<br>mii hô:ng ùun ìik mái? |
| Where can I park the car? | ฉันจะจอดรถได้ที่ไหน<br>chan ja jòrt rót dâai tîi näi? |
| What time is breakfast? | อาหารเช้าเสริฟกี่โมง<br>aa-häan cháao surp gìi moong? |

| | |
|---|---|
| What time is dinner? | อาหารเย็นเสริฟกี่โมง<br>aa-häan yen surp gìi moong? |
| The key, please | ขอกุญแจ<br>kör gun-jae |
| Room number... | ห้องเบอร์...<br>hô:ng bur... |
| Are there any messages for me? | มีข้อความถึงฉันหรือไม่<br>mii kôr-kwaam tüng chan rüu mâi? |
| I'm leaving tomorrow | ฉันจะออกพรุ่งนี้<br>chan ja òrk prûng-níi |
| Please prepare the bill | กรุณาเตรียมบิลไว้ด้วย<br>ga-ru-naa dtriam bill wái dûoy |
| I'd like an early morning call at 7 am. | ฉันต้องการบริการปลุกเจ็ดโมงเช้า<br>chan dtô:ng gaan bo-ri-gaan bplùk jèt moong cháao |

# Shopping

## Shopping phrases

• • • • • • • • • • • • • • • • • • • • • • • • • • • • •

Shopping centres in Bangkok and other big cities are open from 10.00 am to 9.00 pm Monday to Sunday. In most of the shops it is possible to negotiate the price with the seller.

**FACE TO FACE**

**A** ฉันต้องการซื้อชุดสีฟ้า
chan dtô:ng gaan súu chùt-síi-fáa
I would like to buy a blue dress

**B** คุณใส่ขนาดอะไร
khun sài kà-nàat à-rai?
What is your size?

**A** ขนาด 34/32
kà-nàat säam sìp sìi/säam sìp sö:ng
size 34/32

61

| | |
|---|---|
| Where are the shops? | ร้านค้าอยู่ที่ไหน<br>ráan káa yùu tîi näi? |
| I'm looking for... | ฉันมองหา...<br>chan morng häa... |
| Where is the nearest...? | ...ที่ใกล้ที่สุดอยู่ไหน<br>...tîi glâi tîi sut yùu tîi näi? |
| Where is the nearest baker's? | ร้านขนมปังที่ใกล้ที่สุด อยู่ไหน<br>ráan ka-nöm bpang tîi glâi tîi sut yùu tîi näi? |
| Where is the bazaar? | ตลาดนัดอยู่ที่ไหน<br>dtà-làat nat yùu tîi näi? |
| Is it open? | มันเปิดไหม<br>man bpùrt mái? |
| When does it close? | มันปิดเมื่อไหร่<br>man bpìt mûa rai? |
| Can I take that one? | ฉันซื้ออันนี้ได้ไหม<br>chan súu an níi dâai mái? |
| How much is it? | ราคาเท่าไหร่<br>raa-kaa tâo rài? |
| It's too expensive | มันแพงเกินไป<br>man paeng gurn bpai |
| I don't want it | ฉันไม่ต้องการมัน<br>chan mâi dtô:ng gaan man |

# Shops

• • • • • • • • • • • • • • • • • • • • • • • • • • • • • • • • •

| | | |
|---|---|---|
| Where is...? | ...อยู่ที่ไหน | |
| | ...yùu tîi näi? | |
| Where is the baker's? | ร้านขนมปังอยู่ที่ไหน | |
| | ráan ka-nöm bpang yùu tîi näi? | |

| | | |
|---|---|---|
| baker's | ร้านขนมปัง | ráan ka-nöm bpang |
| bookshop | ร้านหนังสือ | ráan näng-süu |
| butcher's | ร้านขายเนื้อสัตว์ | ráan käai núa-sàt |
| cake shop | ร้านเค็ก | ráan kéek |
| clothes shop | ร้านเสื้อผ้า | ráan sûa-pâa |
| electrical goods | ร้านเครื่องไฟฟ้า | ráan krûang fai-fáa |
| fishmonger's | ร้านขายปลา | ráan käai bplaa |
| furniture shop | ร้านเฟอร์นิเจอร์ | ráan fur-ni-jur |
| gifts/ souvenirs | ร้านของที่ระลึก | ráan kö:ng tîi ra-lúk |
| greengrocer's | ร้านขายผัก | ráan käai pàk |
| grocer's | ร้านขายของชำ | ráan käai kö:ng cham |

| hairdresser's | ร้านตัดผม | ráan dtat pŏm |
| jeweller's | ร้านเครื่องเพชร | ráan krûang pét |
| market | ตลาด | dta-làat |
| newsagent | ร้านหนังสือพิมพ์ | ráan năng-sŭu pim |
| optician | ร้านแว่นตา | ráan wâen-dtaa |
| pharmacy | ร้านขายยา | ráan kăai yaa |
| shoe shop | ร้านรองเท้า | ráan ro:ng táao |
| shop | ร้านค้า | ráan káa |
| shopping centre | ห้างสรรพสินค้า | hâang sàp-pa-sĭn-káa |
| spice/herb shop | ร้านเครื่องเทศ | ráan krûang-têet |
| stationer's | ร้านเครื่องเขียน | ráan krûang kĭan |
| supermarket | ซุปเปอร์มาร์เก็ต | sup-bpur-maa-gét |
| tobacconist's | ร้านบุหรี่ | ráan bu-rìi |
| toy shop | ร้านของเล่น | ráan kŏ:ng lên |

# Food (general)

| | | |
|---|---|---|
| bread | ขนมปัง | ka-nŏm bpang |
| butter | เนย | neei |
| cakes | เค้ก | kéek |
| cheese | ขีส | chiis |
| chicken | ไก่ | gài |
| chocolate | ช็อกโกแล็ต | chock-goo-laet |
| coffee (instant) | กาแฟ | gaa-fae |
| coffee | กาแฟเม็ด | gaa-fae-met |
| crisps | มันฝรั่งทอด | man-fa-ràng- tôrt |
| egg | ไข่ | kài |
| fish | ปลา | bplaa |
| flour | แป้ง | bpâeng |
| honey | น้ำผึ้ง | náam-pûng |
| jam | แยม | yaem |
| margarine | เนยเทียม | neei-tiam |
| marmalade | แยมผลไม้ | yaem pönla-máai |
| milk | นม | nom |
| olive oil | น้ำมันมะกอก | náam-man ma-gòrk |
| orange juice | น้ำส้ม | náam sôm |

| pasta | พาสต้า | pass-tâa |
| pepper (seasoning) | พริกไทย | prik-tai |
| rice | ข้าว | kâao |
| salt | เกลือ | glua |
| stock cubes | ก้อนปรุงน้ำแกง | kô:n-bprung-náam-gaeng |
| sugar | น้ำตาล | náam-dtaan |
| tea | ชา | chaa |
| vinegar | น้ำส้มสายชู | náam-sôm-säai-shuu |
| yoghurt | โยเกิร์ต | yoo-gurt |

## Food (fruit and veg)

### Fruit

| apples | แอ็ปเปิ้ล | ab-bpûrn |
| bananas | กล้วย | glûai |
| cherries | เชอรี่ | chur-rii |
| durian | ทุเรียน | tú-rian |

| grapes | องุ่น | a-ngùn |
| lime | มะนาว | ma-nauw |
| longan | ลำไย | lam-yai |
| mango | มะม่วง | má-mûang |
| mangosteen | มังคุด | mang-kút |
| melon | แตงเขียว | dtaeng-kïao |
| nectarines | ลูกท้อ | lûuk-tór |
| oranges | ส้ม | sôm |
| peaches | พีช | peach |
| pears | แพร์ | pear |
| pineapple | สับปะรด | sap-bpa-rod |
| plums | พลัม | plam |
| pomegranate | ทับทิม | tâb-tim |
| rambutan | เงาะ | ngó: |
| strawberries | สตรอเบอรี่ | sa-dtror-bur-rii |
| watermelon | แตงโม | dtaeng-moo |

## Vegetables

| cabbage | กะหล่ำปลี | ga-làm-bplii |
| carrots | แครอท | kae-rò:t |
| cauliflower | ดอกกะหล่ำ | dorg-ka-làm |

| | | |
|---|---|---|
| cucumber | แตงกวา | dtaeng-gwaa |
| garlic | กระเทียม | gra- tiam |
| green beans | ถั่วเขียว | tùa-kïao |
| lettuce | ผักกาดแก้ว | pàk-gaad-gâew |
| mushrooms | เห็ด | hèt |
| onions | หอมใหญ่ | hörm-yai |
| peas | ถั่ว | tùa |
| peppers | พริกไทย | prik-tai |
| potatoes | มันฝรั่ง | man-fa-ràng |
| spinach | ผักโขม | pàk-köom |
| tomatoes | มะเขือเทศ | má-küa-têet |

## Clothes

| women's sizes | | men's suit sizes | | shoe sizes | | | |
|---|---|---|---|---|---|---|---|
| UK | TH | UK | EU | UK | TH | UK | TH |
| 10 | 9 | 36 | 36 | 2 | 5 | 7 | 10 |
| 12 | 11 | 38 | 38 | 3 | 6 | 8 | 11 |
| 14 | 13 | 40 | 40 | 4 | 7 | 9 | 12 |
| 16 | 15 | 42 | 42 | 5 | 8 | 10 | 13 |
| 18 | 17 | 44 | 44 | 6 | 9 | 11 | 14 |
| 20 | 19 | 46 | 46 | | | | |

**FACE TO FACE**

**A** ฉันลองตัวนี้ได้ไหม
chan lorng dtua níi dâai mái?
Can I try this one on?

**B** ได้ครับ/ค่ะ ที่ห้องนี้ครับ/ค่ะ
dâai krab/ká tîi hô:ng níi krab/ká
Yes, of course, you can try it on in here

**A** มีขนาดเล็ก/กลาง/ใหญ่ ไหมครับ/คะ
mii kà-nàat lék/glaang/yài mái krab/ká?
Is there a small/medium/large size for this one?

**B** มีครับ/ค่ะ/ไม่มีครับ/ค่ะ
mii krab/ká/mâi mii krab/ká
Yes, there is/no, there isn't

| | |
|---|---|
| Is it real leather? | หนังแท้ไหม |
| | năng táe mái? |
| Do you have this one in other colours? | อันนี้มีสีอื่นไหม |
| | an-níi mii síi ùun mái? |
| It's too expensive | มันแพงเกินไป |
| | man paeng gurn bpai |
| It's too big | มันใหญ่เกินไป |
| | man yài gurnn bpai |

| It's too small | มันเล็กเกินไป | |
| | man lék gurn bpai | |
| No thanks, I don't want it | ไม่เอา ขอบคุณ ฉันไม่ต้องการมัน | |
| | mâi ao kòrb-kun chan mâi dtô:ng gaan man | |

## Clothes (articles)

| cotton | ผ้าฝ้าย | pâa-fâai |
| leather | หนัง | näng |
| silk | ผ้าไหม | pâa-mäi |
| wool | ขนสัตว์ | kön-sàt |
| coat | เสื้อคลุม | sûa-klum |
| dress | กระโปรงชุด | gra-bproong-shút |
| hat | หมวก | mùak |
| jacket | เสื้อเจ็กเก็ต | sûa-jack-gét |
| knickers | กางเกงในผู้หญิง | gaang-geng-nai-pûu-yïng |
| sandals | รองเท้าแตะ | ro:ng-táo-dtà: |
| shirt | เสื้อ | sûa |

> **Paying** (p 97)

| | | |
|---|---|---|
| shorts | กางเกงขาสั้น | gaang-geng-käa-sân |
| skirt | กระโปรง | gra-bproong |
| socks | ถุงเท้า | tüng-táo |
| swimsuit | ชุดว่ายน้ำ | shút-wâai-náam |
| t-shirt | เสื้อยืด | sûa-yûud |
| trousers | กางเกงขายาว | gaang-geng-käa-yao |
| underpants | กางเกงใน | gaang-geng-nai |

# Maps and guides

You can get a free copy of a map of Thailand and
some big-city maps at the TAT (Tourism Authority of
Thailand) counter at the airport. Some big hotels
also provide free city maps for their customers.

| | |
|---|---|
| Where can I buy a map? | ฉันจะซื้อแผนที่ได้ที่ไหน<br>chan ja súu päen-tîi dâai tîi nái? |
| Do you have a road map? | คุณมีแผนที่ของถนนไหม<br>khun mii päen-tîi kö:ng tà-nön mái? |
| Do you have a town plan? | คุณมีผังเมืองไหม<br>khun mii päng muang mái? |

71

| Do you have a leaflet/ guidebook in English? | คุณมีคู่มือแนะนำการท่อง เที่ยวไหม |
| | khun mii kûu-muu naé-nam gaan tô:ng-tîao mái? |
| Can you show me where ... is on the map? | คุณช่วยบอกผม/ดิฉัน หน่อยว่า ... อยู่ตรงไหนบนแผนที่ |
| | khun chûai bòrk pöm/di-chan nò:i wâa ... yùu dtrong näi bon päen-tîi? |
| Where can I buy a newspaper? | ฉันจะซื้อหนังสือพิมพ์ได้ที่ ไหน |
| | chan ja súu näng-süu pim dâai tîi näi? |
| Have you any English newspapers? | คุณมีหนังสือพิมพ์ภาษา อังกฤษไหม |
| | khun mii näng-süu pim paa-säa ang-grìt mái? |

> **Asking the way** (p 30)
> **Sightseeing and tourist office** (p 76)

# Post office

Post offices which are run by the government are open from 8.30 am to 3.30 pm, Monday to Friday. Some big hotels offer mailing services which cost a little more. There are also some other private companies such as FedEx and UPS which offer faster services, and have longer business hours.

| ทางอากาศ<br>taang- aa- gàat | airmail |
|---|---|
| ต่างประเทศ<br>dtàang bpra têet | overseas |
| ในประเทศ   nai bpra-têet | inland |
| ในพื้นที่   nai púun-tîi | local |
| จดหมาย   jòt- mäai | letter |
| ไปรษณียบัตร<br>prai-sa-nii-ya-bàt | postcard |
| แสตมป์   sà-dtaem | stamps |

| Where is the post office? | ไปรษณีย์อยู่ที่ไหน |
| | bprai-sa-nii yùu tîi nǎi? |
| Where can I buy stamps? | ฉันจะซื้อแสตมป์ได้ที่ไหน |
| | chan ja súu sà-dtaem dâai tîi nǎi? |
| 5 stamps | แสตมป์ห้าดวง |
| | sà-dtaem hâa duang |
| 10 stamps | แสตมป์สิบดวง |
| | sà-dtaem sìp duang |
| for postcards | สำหรับไปรษณียบัตร |
| | sǎm-ràp prai-sa-nii-ya-bàt |
| for letters | สำหรับจดหมาย |
| | sǎm-ràp jòt-mǎai |
| to Britain | ส่งไปอังกฤษ |
| | sòng bpai ang-grìt |
| to America | ส่งไปอเมริกา |
| | sòng bpai a-may-ri-gaa |
| to Australia | ส่งไปออสเตรเลีย |
| | sòng bpai o:s-dtray-lia |

> **Money** (p 96) > **Paying** (p 97)

# Photos

......................................................

| Where is a photographic shop? | ร้านถ่ายภาพอยู่ที่ไหน |
| | ráan tàai-pâap yùu tîi nǎi? |
| I need a film for this camera | ฉันต้องการฟิล์มสีสำหรับกล้องถ่ายรูปอันนี้ |
| | chan dtô:ng-gaan film sǐi säm-räp klô:ng tàai ruub an níi |
| I need batteries for this | ฉันต้องการแบ็ตเตอรี่สำหรับสิ่งนี้ |
| | chan dtô:ng-gaan baet-dtur-rìi säm-räp sìng níi |
| I'd like these films developed | ฉันต้องการล้างรูปและอัดภาพ |
| | chan dtô:ng-gaan láang ruub laé àt pâap |
| How long will it take? | จะใช้เวลานานเท่าไหร่ |
| | ja chái wee-laa naan tâo rài? |
| How much will it cost? | ราคาเท่าไหร่ |
| | raa-kaa tâo rài? |

# Leisure

## Sightseeing and tourist office

Tourist offices provide lists of accommodation, maps and leaflets describing local attractions.

| | |
|---|---|
| ข้อมูล kôr-moon | information |
| สำนักงานการ ท่องเที่ยว säm-nak-ngaan-gaan- tô:ng tîao | tourist office |
| พิพิธภัณฑ์ pí-pít-ta-pan | museum |
| ห้องแสดงศิลปะ hô:ng sa-daeng sïn-lá-bpà | art gallery |
| วัด wát | temple |
| ทัวร์นำเที่ยว tuaa-nam-tîao | guided tour |

| ตั๋ว | dtüa | tickets |
| ห้องสุขา | hô:ng su-käa | toilet |

| Where is the tourist office? | สำนักงานการท่องเที่ยวอยู่ที่ไหน |
| | säm-nak-ngaan-gaan- tô:ng tîao yùu tîi näi? |
| What can we visit in the area? | บริเวณนั้นมีอะไรบ้าง |
| | bo:-ri-ween nán mii a-rai bâang? |
| Have you got details in English? | มีรายละเอียดเป็นภาษาอังกฤษไหม |
| | mii raai là-ìat bpen paa-säa ang-grìt mái? |
| Are there any excursions? | มีโปรแกรมเที่ยวระยะสั้นไหม |
| | mii bpro-graem tîao rá-yá sân mái? |
| When does it leave? | จะไปเมื่อไหร่ |
| | ja bpai mûa-rai? |
| When does it get back? | จะกลับเมื่อไหร่ |
| | ja glàb mûa-rai? |

Sightseeing and tourist office

> **Maps and guides** (p 71)

# Entertainment

| | |
|---|---|
| What is there to do in the evenings? | มีอะไรที่น่าทำตอนเย็นบาง |
| | mii à-rai tîi nâa tam dto:n yen bâang? |
| We would like to go to a disco | เราต้องการไปเธค |
| | rao dtông gaan bpai tek |
| Is there anywhere we can go to hear live music? | ที่ไหนมีการแสดงดนตรีสดบาง |
| | tîi näi mii gaan sa-daeng don-dtrii sòt bâang? |
| Is there anywhere we can go to see Thai dancing? | ที่ไหนมีการแสดงรำไทยบาง |
| | tîi näi mii gaan-sa-daeng ram-tai bâang? |
| Is there any entertainment for children? | ที่ไหนมีความบันเทิงสำหรับเด็ก |
| | tîi näi mii kwaam ban-turng säm-räp dèk? |

78

# Leisure/beach

. . . . . . . . . . . . . . . . . . . . . . . . . . . . . . . . . . . . .

| ชายหาด chaai-hàat | beach |
| อันตราย an-dta-raai | danger |
| ฝักบัว fàk bua | showers |

Are there any good beaches round here?
: แถวนี้มีหาดสวย สวย บ้างไหม
: täew níi mii hàat süai süai bâang mái?

Is there a bus (shared taxi) to the beach?
: มีรถบัส (รถประจำทาง) ไปชายหาดไหม
: mii rót bás (rót-bpra-jam-taang) bpai chaai-hàat mái?

Can we go windsurfing?
: เราเล่นกระดานโต้คลื่น ได้ไหม
: rao lên grà daan dtôo klûun dâai mái?

Please go away!
: กรุณาอย่ารบกวนครับ/ค่ะ
: ga-ru-naa yàa róp-guan krab/kà!

# Music

. . . . . . . . . . . . . . . . . . . . . . . . . . . . . . . .

| | |
|---|---|
| Is there anywhere we can go to hear music? | เราจะไปฟังเพลงได้ที่ไหนบ้าง<br>rao ja bpai fang pleeng dâai tîi nǎi bâang? |
| Are there any concerts? | ที่ไหนมีคอนเสิร์ตบ้าง<br>tîi nǎi mii ko:n-surt bâang? |
| Where can I get tickets? | ฉันจะซื้อตั๋วได้ที่ไหนบ้าง<br>chan ja súu dtǔa dâai tîi nǎi bâang? |
| Where can I hear some classical music/jazz? | ฉันจะไปฟังเพลงคลาสสิก/เพลงแจ๊ส ได้ที่ไหนบ้าง<br>chan ja bpai fang pleeng clas-sic/jass dâai tîi nǎi bâang? |

# Cinema

. . . . . . . . . . . . . . . . . . . . . . . . . . . . . . . .

| | | |
|---|---|---|
| โรงหนัง | roong-nǎng | cinema |
| ฉาย | chǎai | screening |

> **Making friends** (p 24)

| What's on at the cinema? | มีหนังอะไรฉายบ้าง |
| --- | --- |
| | mii näng à-rai chäai bâang? |
| What time does the film start? | หนังฉายกี่โมง |
| | näng chäai gìi moong? |
| How much are the tickets? | ตั๋วหนังราคาเท่าไหร่ |
| | dtüa näng raa-kaa tâo rài? |
| Two for (give name and time of performance) showing | ตั๋วสองใบเรื่อง... |
| | dtüa sö:ng bai rûang... |

**YOU MAY HEAR...**

หนังเรื่อง ...
ตั๋วหมดแล้วครับ/ค่ะ
näng rûang ... dtüa mòt láew krab/ká

For screening ... we have no tickets left

# Temple

Dress appropriately when you go to the temples. Never wear sleeveless tops, shorts or short skirts, as you will not be allowed in. Shoes have to be taken off once inside the chapel where the principal image of Buddha is kept. Do not climb onto the

81

Buddha image to take a photograph or do anything that may indicate a lack of respect.

Buddhist monks are forbidden to touch or be touched by a woman. If a woman has to give anything to a monk, she should ask a man to pass it to the monk. If there is not a man around, the monk will put a cloth on a table, and then the woman can place the item on the cloth.

|  |  |
|---|---|
| วัด  wát | temple |
| ศาสนาพุทธ sàat-sà-näa-put | Buddhist |
| ศาสนาคริสต์ sàat-sà-näa-kris | Christian |
| รองเท้า  ro:ng-táao | shoes |
| ห้ามถ่ายภาพ hâam tàai-pâap | no photos |
| ห้ามถ่ายวิดีโอ hâam tàai video | no videos |

| | |
|---|---|
| I'd like to see the temple | ฉันต้องการไปดูวัด chan dtô:ng gaan bpai duu wát |

| When can we see the temple? | เมื่อไหร่เราจะได้ไปวัด |
|---|---|
| | mûa-rai rao ja dâai bpai wát? |
| Where is the temple? | วัดอยู่ที่ไหน |
| | wát yùu tîi näi? |

## Television

. . . . . . . . . . . . . . . . . . . . . . . . . . . . . . . . . . . . . . .

The state channel TRT3 has the news in English, German and French and some films with original language subtitles. Most of the hotels and bars have a satellite dish.

| รีโมทคอนโทรล rii mòot ko:n trool | remote control |
|---|---|
| ข่าว kàao | news |
| เปิดทีวี bpùrd tii-vii | to switch on |
| ปิดทีวี bpìd tii-vii | to switch off |
| การ์ตูน gaar-tuun | cartoons |

| Where is the television? | โทรทัศน์อยู่ไหน |
| | too-rà-tát yùu näi? |
| How do I switch on the television? | ฉันจะเปิดทีวีได้อย่างไร |
| | chan ja bpùrd tii-vii dâai yàang rai? |
| What's on television? | มีรายการทีวีอะไรบ้าง |
| | mii raai-gaan tii-vii a-rai bâang? |
| Are there any English-speaking channels? | มีช่องไหนที่เป็นภาษา อังกฤษบ้าง |
| | mii chô:ng näi tîi bpen paa-säa ang-grìt bâang? |
| Are there any children's programmes? | มีช่องไหนที่มีรายการเด็ก บ้าง |
| | mii ch ô:ng näi tîi mii raai-gaan dèk bâang? |
| When is the football/news on? | เมื่อไหร่จะมีรายการ ฟุตบอล/รายการข่าว |
| | mûa-rai ja mii raai-gaan fut-bo:n/ raai-gaan kàao? |

84

# Sport

| | |
|---|---|
| Where can we play tennis/golf/football? | เราจะไปเล่นเทนนิส/กอล์ฟ/ฟุตบอล ได้ที่ไหน<br>rao ja bpai lên ten-nïs/go:f/fut-bo:n dâai tîi nái? |
| Can we play tennis/golf? | เราเล่นเทนนิส/กอล์ฟ ได้ไหม<br>rao lên ten-nïs/go:f dâai mái? |
| Can we hire rackets/golf clubs? | เราเช่าไม้เทนนิส/ไมกอล์ฟ ได้ไหม<br>rao châo mái ten-nïs/mái go:f dâai mái? |
| How much is it per hour? | ชั่วโมงละเท่าไหร่<br>chûa-moong lá tâo-rài? |
| Can we watch a football match? | ให้เราดูรายการฟุตบอล ได้ไหม<br>hâi rao duu raai-gaan fut-bo:n dâai mái? |
| Where can we get tickets? | เราจะซื้อตั๋วได้ที่ไหน<br>rao ja súu dtüa dâai tîi nái? |

| How do we get to the stadium? | เราจะไปสนามกีฬาได้ อย่างไร |
| | rao ja bpai sà-năam gii-laa dâai yàang-rai? |

# Walking

. . . . . . . . . . . . . . . . . . . . . . . . . . . . . . . . . . . . . . .

| Are there any guided walks? | มีทัวร์นำเดินเที่ยวไหม |
| | mii tuaa nam durn-tîaw mái? |
| Do you have a guide to local walks? | คุณมีคู่มือเดินเที่ยวใน พื้นที่ไหม |
| | khun mii kûu-muu durn-tîaw nai púun-tîi mái? |
| How many kilometres is the walk? | ระยะทางเดินกี่กิโลเมตร |
| | rá-yá taang durn gìi gi-loo-met? |
| How long will it take? | ใช้เวลานานเท่าไหร่ |
| | chái wee-laa naan tâo rài? |
| Is it very steep? | ทางชันมากไหม |
| | taang chan mâak mái? |
| I'd like to go climbing | ฉันต้องการไปปีนเขา |
| | chan dtô:ng gaan bpai bpiin kăo |

> **Maps and guides** (p 71)

# Communications

## Telephone and mobile

A phonecard is the most convenient way to make
an international call. To call from Thailand to the UK
dial **00**, and then **44**, followed by the area code.
To call from the UK to Thailand dial **00**, and then
**66**, followed by the area code. For example,
Bangkok's area code is **2**, so you dial **00-662-
phone number**. Call **1313** for the phone directory.

| | |
|---|---|
| เหรียญโทรศัพท์<br>rĭan too-rá-sàp | phone token |
| บัตรโทรศัพท์<br>bàt too-rá-sàp | phonecard |
| หนังสือโทรศัพท์<br>năng-sŭu too-rá-sàp | telephone directory |
| เก็บเงินปลายทาง<br>gèb ngurn bplaai taang | reverse charges<br>(collect) |

| รหัสโทรศัพท์<br>rà-hàt too-rá-sàp | dialling code |
|---|---|

Hello, I am... — สวัสดีครับ/ค่ะ ผม/ดิฉัน...
sa-wad-dii krab/ka pöm/
di-chan...

I would like to speak to... — ผม/ดิฉัน
ต้องการพูดกับคุณ...
pöm/di-chan dtô:ng gaan pûud
gàb khun...

I want to make a phone call — ฉันต้องการใช้โทรศัพท์
chan dtô:ng gaan chái too-rá-sàp

I want to phone the UK — ฉันต้องการโทรฯไปอังกฤษ
chan dtô:ng gaan too bpai ang-grìt

An outside line, please — ต่อสายนอกครับ/ค่ะ
dtòr säai nôrk krab/ka

Where can I buy a phonecard? — ฉันจะซื้อบัตรโทรศัพท์ได้
ที่ไหน
chan ja súu bàt too-rá-sàp dâai tîi
näi?

Please write the phone number down — กรุณาจดเบอร์โทรศัพท์
ga-ru-naa jòd bur too-rá-sàp

| | |
|---|---|
| Do you have a mobile phone? | คุณมีโทรศัพท์มือถือไหม<br>khun mii too-rá-sàp muu tüu mái? |
| Can I speak to... | ฉันต้องการพูดกับ...<br>chan dtô:ng gaan pûud kàb... |
| This is... | นี้คือ...<br>níi kuu... |
| I'll call back later | ฉันจะโทรกลับมาใหม่<br>chan ja too klàb maa mài |
| I'll call again tomorrow | ฉันจะโทรมาใหม่พรุ่งนี้<br>chan ja too maa mài prûng níi |

### YOU MAY HEAR...

| | |
|---|---|
| สวัสดีครับ/ค่ะ<br>sa-wad-dii krab/kà | Hello |
| กรุณาถือสายรอสักครู่<br>ga-ru-naa tüu säai ror sak-krûu | Please hold on |
| ใครโทรมา<br>krai too maa? | Who is calling? |
| คุณโทรกลับมาใหม่<br>ได้ไหมครับ/ค่ะ<br>khun too glàb maa mài dâai mái krab/kà? | Can you call back later? |

| คุณต้องการทิ้งข้อความไว้ไหม<br>khun dtô:ng gaan tíng kôr-kwaam wâi mái? | Do you want to leave a message? |
| คุณโทรเบอร์ผิด<br>khun too bur pìd | Wrong number |

## Text messaging

........................................

SMS has become popular in Thailand.

| I will text you | ฉันจะส่งข้อความถึงคุณ<br>chan ja sòng kôr-kwaam tüng khun |
| Can you text me? | คุณจะส่งข้อความถึงฉันได้ไหม<br>khun ja sòng kôr-kwaam tüng chan dâai mái? |
| Did you get my text message? | คุณได้รับข้อความของฉันไหม<br>khun dâai ráb kôr-kwaam kö:ng chan mái? |

| | |
|---|---|
| Can you send me a picture from your mobile? | คุณสามารถส่งรูปจาก โทรศัพท์มือถือของคุณได้ หรือไม่ |
| | khun säa-mâat sòng rûub jàak too-rá-sàp muu tüu kö:ng khun dâai rüu mâi? |
| Hello | สวัสดีครับ/ค่ะ |
| | sa-wad-dii krab/kà |
| Hello (to answer the phone) | สวัสดีครับ/ค่ะ |
| | sa-wad-dii krab/kà |
| See you | แล้วเจอกัน |
| | láew jur gan |
| tomorrow | พรุ่งนี้ |
| | prûng níi |
| please call me | กรุณาโทรถึงผม/ดิฉัน |
| | ga-ru-naa too tüng pöm/di-chan |
| today | วันนี้ |
| | wan níi |
| too late | สายเกินไป |
| | säai gurn bpai |
| tonight | คืนนี้ |
| | kuun níi |
| text me | ส่งข้อความถึงฉัน |
| | sòng kôr-kwaam tüng chan |

91

| Free to talk? | ว่างที่จะคุยไหม |
| | wâang tîi ja kui mái? |
| I'll call you back later | ฉันจะโทรฯถึงคุณทีหลัง |
| | chan ja too tŭng khun tii läng |
| Thanks | ขอบคุณ |
| | kòrb kun |
| Are you OK? | เป็นอะไรหรือเปล่า |
| | bpen a-rai rüu bplàao? |

# E-mail

. . . . . . . . . . . . . . . . . . . . . . . . . . . . . . . . . . . . . .

The TLD (internet suffix) for Thailand is **.co.th**

| Do you have e-mail? | คุณมีอีเมล์ไหม |
| | khun mii e-mail mái? |
| My e-mail address is... | อีเมล์ของฉัน... |
| | e-mail kö:ng chan... |
| What is your e-mail address? | อะไรคืออีเมล์ของคุณ |
| | a-rai kuu e-mail kö:ng khun? |
| How do you spell it? | สะกดยังไง |
| | sà-gòt yang ngai? |
| All one word | เขียนติดกันหมด |
| | kĭan dtìd gan mòt |

| | |
|---|---|
| All lower case | เขียนด้วเล็กหมด |
| | kian dtua lék mòt |
| Can I send an e-mail? | ฉันจะส่งอีเมล์ได้ไหม |
| | chan ja sòng e-mail dâai mái? |
| Did you get my e-mail? | คุณได้รับอีเมล์ของฉันไหม |
| | khun dâai ráb e-mail kö:ng chan mái? |

## Internet

It is easy to find an Internet café in Bangkok. In other cities, you will find an Internet service in the big hotels.

| | |
|---|---|
| โฮมเพจ  hoom-pèij | home |
| ชื่อผู้ใช้  chûu pûu chái | username |
| ค้นหา  kón-häa | to browse |
| เครื่องค้นหา krûang kón-häa | search engine |
| รหัส  rá-hàt | password |
| ติดต่อเรา  dtìd-dtòr rao | contact us |

| กลับไปที่รายการเลือก<br>klàb bpai tîi raai-gaan lûak | back to menu |
| แผนที่เว็บไซต์<br>păen-tîi web site | sitemap |

| Are there any Internet cafés here? | มีอินเดอร์เน็ตคาเฟ่ที่ไหน<br>บาง<br>mii in-ter-net kaa-fè tîi năi bâang? |
| How much is it to log on for an hour? | ค่าบริการชั่วโมงละ<br>เท่าไหร<br>kâa bo:-ri-gaan chûa-moong lá tâo rài? |
| I would like to print some pages | ฉันต้องการจะพิมพ์บาง<br>หนา<br>chan dtô:ng gaan ja pìm baang nâa |

## Fax

. . . . . . . . . . . . . . . . . . . . . . . . . . . . . . . . . . . . . . . .

You can find fax services at hotels. In the big cities, you also can find fax services at travel agencies.

## Addressing a fax

| | | |
|---|---|---|
| จาก | jàak | from |
| ถึง | tüng | to |
| วันที่ | wan-tĩi | date |
| ...หน้ารวมทั้งหน้านี้ | | ...pages including this |
| ...nâa ruam-táng nâa níi | | one |

| | |
|---|---|
| I want to send a fax | ฉันต้องการส่งแฟ็กซ์ |
| | chan dtô:ng gaan sòng fax |
| Do you have a fax? | คุณมีแฟ็กซ์ไหม |
| | khun mii fax mái? |
| Where can I send a fax? | ฉันจะส่งแฟ็กซ์ได้ที่ไหน |
| | chan ja sòng fax dâai tĩi näi? |
| How much is it to send a fax? | ค่าส่งแฟ็กซ์เท่าไหร่ |
| | kâa sòng fax tâo rài? |
| What is your fax number? | แฟ็กซ์ของคุณหมายเลข อะไร |
| | fax kö:ng khun mäai-lêek a-rai? |
| The fax number is... | หมายเลขแฟ็กซ์... |
| | mäai-lêek fax... |

# Practicalities

## Money

Banking hours are 8.30 am to 3.00 pm, Monday to Friday. Some branches located in shopping centres have longer business hours, some being open from 10.00 am to 9.00 pm. The Thai currency is the **Baht**.

| | |
|---|---|
| Where is the nearest bank? | ธนาคารที่ใกล้ที่สุดอยู่ที่ไหน |
| | ta-naa-kaan tîi glâi tîi-sùt yùu tîi näi? |
| Where is the nearest currency office? | ที่รับแลกเงินที่ใกล้ที่สุดอยู่ที่ไหน |
| | tîi ráb lâek-ngurn tîi glâi tîi-sùt yùu tîi näi? |
| Can I change money here? | ฉันแลกเงินที่นี่ได้ไหม |
| | chan lâek ngurn tîi nîi dâai mái? |
| What is the exchange rate? | อัตราแลกเปลี่ยนเท่าไหร่ |
| | àt-dtraa lâek bplìan tâo rài? |

| I want to change £50 | ฉันต้องการแลก ห้าสิบ ปอนด์ |
|---|---|
| | chan dtô:ng gaan lâek hâa-sìp bporn |
| I want to buy traveller's cheques (only at banks) | ฉันต้องการซื้อเช็ค เดินทาง |
| | chan dtô:ng gaan súu check durn-taang |

## Paying

· · · · · · · · · · · · · · · · · · · · · · · · · · · · · · · · · · · ·

Credit card payments are accepted; however, a 3% handling fee is added for using them. Service charge in restaurants, bars and cafés is included in the bill.

| ใบเก็บเงิน  bai- gèb ngurn | bill |
|---|---|
| ใบเสร็จ  bai-sèt | receipt |
| ใบส่งของ  bai- sòng-kö:ng | invoice |
| โต๊ะเก็บเงิน  dtó- gèb ngurn | cash desk |
| เครดิตการ์ด  krei-dit-gáat | credit card |

| I'd like to pay now | ฉันต้องการจ่ายเงิน |
| | chan dtô:ng gaan jàai ngurn |
| How much is it? | ทั้งหมดเท่าใหร่ |
| | táng mòt tâo rài? |
| Can I pay...? | ฉันใช้ ... จ่ายได้ใหม |
| | chan chái ... jàai dâai mái? |
| Can I pay by credit card/cheque? | ฉันใช้เครดิตการ์ด/เช็คจ่ายได้ใหม |
| | chan chái kree-dit-gáat/check jàai dâai mái? |
| by credit card | ใช้เครดิตการ์ดจ่าย |
| | chái kree-dit-gáat jàai |
| with traveller's cheques | ใช้เช็คเดินทางจ่าย |
| | chái check durn-taang jàai |
| Where do I pay? | จ่ายเงินที่ใหน |
| | jàai ngurn tîi näi? |
| Please write down the price | เขียนราคาให้หน่อย |
| | kïan raa-kaa hâi nòi |
| Put it on my bill (in a hotel) | คิดรวมกับค่าที่พักของฉัน |
| | kìd ruam gàb kâa tîi-pák kö:ng chan |
| I'd like a receipt, please | ขอใบเสร็จด้วยครับ/ค่ะ |
| | kör bai-sèt dûoy krab/ká |

| I think there is a mistake | ฉันคิดว่าคุณคิดตังค์ผิด |
| | chan kíd wâa khun kíd dtang pìd |
| Keep the change | ไม่ต้องคืนเงินทอนครับ/ค่ะ |
| | mâi dtô:ng kuun ngurn-torn krab/ká |

# Luggage

| กระเป๋าเดินทาง<br>grà-bpǎo-durn-taang | suitcase |
| --- | --- |
| กระเป๋าถือ<br>grà-bpǎo-tǔu | handbag |
| กระเป๋าเอกสาร<br>grà-bpǎo èek-gà-sǎen | briefcase |
| กระเป๋าเดินทางเล็ก<br>grà-bpǎo-durn-taang-lék | hand luggage |
| ที่ติดต่อสัมภาระหาย<br>tîi dtid-dtòr sǎm-paa-rá hǎai | left-luggage office |
| ที่เก็บของ    tîi gèb kǒ:ng | locker |
| ที่ลากของ    tîi lâag kǒ:ng | trolley |

> **Shopping** (p 61)

| | |
|---|---|
| My suitcase hasn't arrived | กระเป๋าเดินทางของฉันยัง มาไม่ถึง |
| | grà-bpäo-durn-taang kö:ng chan yang maa mâi tüng |
| My suitcase is missing | กระเป๋าเดินทางของฉัน หายไป |
| | grà-bpäo-durn-taang kö:ng chan häai bpai |
| My suitcase is damaged | กระเป๋าเดินทางของฉัน เสียหาย |
| | grà-bpäo-durn-taang kö:ng chan sïa häai |
| Can I leave my suitcase here? | ฉันจะวางกระเป๋าเดินทาง ตรงนี้ได้ไหม |
| | chan ja waang grà-bpäo-durn-taang dtrong níi dâai mái? |
| Is there a left-luggage office? | ที่ติดต่อสัมภาระหาย อยู่ไหน |
| | tïi dtid-dtòr säm-paa-rá häai yùu näi? |
| When does it open? | มันเปิดเมื่อไหร่ |
| | man bpùrd mûa-rài? |
| When does it close? | มันปิดเมื่อไหร่ |
| | man bpìd mûa-rài? |

# Repairs

. . . . . . . . . . . . . . . . . . . . . . . . .

| ร้านซ่อมรองเท้า<br>ráan sô:m ro:ng-táao | shoe repair shop |
|---|---|
| ร้านซ่อม รอรับได้<br>ráan sô:m ror ráb dâai | repairs while you wait |

| | |
|---|---|
| This is broken | อันนี้เสีย<br>an níi sĭa |
| Where can I get this repaired? | ฉันจะซ่อมอันนี้ได้ที่ไหน<br>chan ja sô:m an níi dâai tîi năi? |
| Can you repair...? | คุณจะซ่อม ... ได้ไหม<br>khun ja sô:m ... dâai mái? |
| my glasses? | แว่นตาของฉัน<br>wâen-dtaa kö:ng chan? |
| my camera? | กล้องถ่ายรูปของฉัน<br>glô:ng tàai ruub kö:ng chan? |
| How much will it cost? | มันราคาเท่าไหร่<br>man raa-kaa tâo rài? |
| How long will it take? | ใช้เวลานานเท่าไหร่<br>chái wee-laa naan tâo rài? |

> **Train** (p 38) > **Air travel** (p 44)

| อันนี้ซ่อมไม่ได้<br>an níi sô:m mâi dâai | I cannot repair this |
| --- | --- |

# Laundry

. . . . . . . . . . . . . . . . . . . . . . . . . . . . . .

| ผงซักฟอก<br>pöng-sák-fôrk | washing powder |
| --- | --- |
| ที่ซักผ้า    tîi sák pâa | launderette |
| บริการซักแห้ง<br>bo:-ri-gaan sák hâeng | dry-cleaner's |

| Where can I wash some clothes? | ฉันจะซักเสื้อผ้าได้ที่ไหน<br>chan ja sák sûa-pâa dâai tîi näi? |
| --- | --- |
| Do you have a laundry service? | คุณมีบริการซักผ้าไหม<br>khun mii bo:-ri-gaan sák pâa mái? |
| Where is the launderette? | ที่ซักผ้าอยู่ที่ไหน<br>tîi sák pâa yùu tîi näi? |
| Where is the dry-cleaner's? | บริการซักแห้งอยู่ที่ไหน<br>bo:-ri-gaan sák hâeng yùu tîi näi? |

> **Breakdown** (p 51)

Practicalities

| Can I borrow an iron? | ให้ฉันยืมเตารีดได้ไหม |
| | hâi chan yuum dtao-rîid dâai mái? |

**YOU MAY HEAR...**

| ต่อชิ้น | per item |
| dtòr chín | |

## Complaints

. . . . . . . . . . . . . . . . . . . . . . . . . . . . . . . . . . . . . . . . .

| This doesn't work | มันไม่ทำงาน |
| | man mâi tam-ngaan |
| The room is dirty | ห้องสกปรก |
| | hô:ng sok-gà-bpròk |
| The room is too hot | ห้องร้อนเกินไป |
| | hô:ng rórn gurn bpai |
| I didn't order this | ฉันไม่ได้สั่งอันนี้ |
| | chan mâi dâai sàng an níi |
| I want to complain... | ฉันต้องการต่อว่า... |
| | chan dtô:ng gaan dtòr-wâa... |
| Please call the manager | กรุณาเรียกผู้จัดการมา |
| | ga-ru-naa rîak pûu-jàt-gaan maa |

| ...out of order | ...ปิดซ่อม |
| | ...bpid sô:m |
| toilet | ห้องสุขา |
| | hô:ng su-käa |
| shower | ห้องอาบน้ำ |
| | hô:ng àap náam |
| television | โทรทัศน์ |
| | too-rà-tát |

## Problems

. . . . . . . . . . . . . . . . . . . . . . . . . . . . .

| Can you help me? | คุณจะช่วยฉันได้ไหม |
| | khun ja chûai chan dâai mái? |
| I don't speak Thai | ฉันไม่สามารถพูดภาษา ไทย |
| | chan mâi säa-mâat pûud paa-säa thai |
| Do you speak English? | คุณพูดภาษาอังกฤษ ได้ไหม |
| | khun pûud paa-säa ang-grìt dâai mái? |

> **Hotel desk** (p 59)

Practicalities

| | |
|---|---|
| Is there someone who speaks English? | มีใครพูดภาษาอังกฤษได้ ไหม |
| | mii krai pûud paa-säa ang-grìt dâai mái? |
| I'm lost | ฉันหลงทาง |
| | chan löng taang |
| I need to go to... | ฉันต้องการจะไป... |
| | chan dtô:ng gaan ja bpai... |
| the station | ที่สถานี |
| | tîi sà-täa-nii |
| my hotel | ที่โรงแรม |
| | tîi roong-raem |
| this address | ที่อยู่นี้ |
| | tîi yùu níi |
| I've missed my train/bus/plane | ฉันพลาดรถไฟ/รถเมล์/ เครื่องบิน |
| | chan plâad rót fai/rót meey/ krûang bin |
| I've missed the connection | ฉันต่อเครื่องไม่ทัน |
| | chan dtòr krûang mâi tan |
| The coach has left without me | รถโค้ชออกไปก่อนฉันจะ มาถึง |
| | rót coach òrk bpai gò:n chan ja maa tüng |

| How does this work? | ทำอย่างไร |
| tam yàang-rai? |
| That man is following me | ผู้ชายคนนั้นตามฉันมา |
| pûu-chaai kon nàn dtaam chan maa |
| I lost my money | ฉันทำเงินหาย |
| chan tam ngurn häai |

# Emergencies

| ตำรวจ  dtam-rùat | police |
|---|---|
| ตำรวจดับเพลิง<br>dtam-rùat dàp-plurng | fire brigade |
| รถพยาบาล<br>rót-pa-yaa-baan | ambulance |
| โรงพยาบาล<br>roong pa-yaa-baan | hospital |

| Help! | ช่วยด้วย |
| | chûai dûoy! |
| Fire! | ไฟไหม้ |
| | fai mâi! |
| There's been an accident | มีอุบัติเหตุ |
| | mii ù-bàt-dtì-hèet |
| Please help me | กรุณาช่วยฉันด้วย |
| | ga-ru-naa chûai chan dûoy |
| Please call the police/fire brigade | ช่วยโทรฯเรียกตำรวจ/ ตำรวจดับเพลิง ด้วย |
| | chûai too ríak dtam-rùat/ dtam-rùat dàp-plurng dûoy |
| Someone has been injured | มีคนบาดเจ็บ |
| | mii kon bàat jèb |
| Where is the police station? | สถานีตำรวจอยู่ไหน |
| | sà-täa-nii dtam-rùat yùu näi? |
| I've been robbed | ฉันถูกปล้น |
| | chan tùuk bplôn |
| I've been raped | ฉันถูกข่มขืน |
| | chan tùuk kòm-küun |
| I want to speak to a policewoman | ฉันต้องการพูดกับตำรวจผู้ หญิง |
| | chan dtô:ng gaan pûud gàb dtam-rùat pûu-ying |

| | |
|---|---|
| Someone has stolen... | มีคนโขมย... <br> mii kon kà-mooi... |
| I've lost... | ...ของฉันหาย <br> ...kö:ng chan häai |
| my money | เงินของฉัน <br> ngurn kö:ng chan |
| my passport | หนังสือเดินทางของฉัน <br> näng-süu-durn-taang kö:ng chan |
| my plane ticket | ตั๋วเครื่องบินของฉัน <br> dtüa krûang bin kö:ng chan |
| My son is missing | ลูกชายของฉันหายไป <br> lûuk-chaai kö:ng chan häai bpai |
| My daughter is missing | ลูกสาวของฉันหายไป <br> lûuk-säao kö:ng chan häai bpai |
| His/Her name is... | ชื่อของเขา... <br> chûu kö:ng kao... |
| I need a report for my insurance | ฉันต้องรายงานบริษัทประกัน <br> chan dtô:ng raai-ngaan bò:-ri-sàt bpra-gan |
| Please call the British Embassy | กรุณาโทรฯไปสถานทูตอังกฤษให้หน่อยครับ/ค่ะ <br> ga-ru-naa too bpai sa-täan-tûut ang-grìt hâi nòi krab/kà |

108

# Health

## Pharmacy

· · · · · · · · · · · · · · · · · · · · · · · · · · ·

Pharmacies ร้านขายยา ráan käai yaa **are open
from 9.00 am to 9.00 pm.**

| | |
|---|---|
| Where is the nearest pharmacy? | ร้านขายยาที่ใกล้ที่สุด<br>อยู่ไหน<br>ráan käai yaa tîi glâi tîi sut yùun näi? |
| I need something... | ฉันต้องการ...<br>chan dtôːng gaan... |
| for diarrhoea | ยาแก้ท้องเสีย<br>yaa gâe tóːng sïa |
| for constipation | ท้องผูก<br>óːng pùuk |
| for food poisoning | สำหรับอาหารเป็นพิษ<br>säm-ràp aa-häan bpen pít |
| Is it safe for...? | มันปลอดภัยสำหรับ ...<br>ไหม<br>man bplòrt pai säm-ràp ... mái? |

109

| children | เด็ก |
| | dèk |
| I am pregnant | ฉันกำลังท้อง |
| | chan gamlang tó:ng |
| What is the dose? | ต้องกินยาอย่างไร |
| | dtô:ng gin yaa yàang rai? |

| กินสามครั้งต่อวัน<br>gin säam kráng dtòr wan | 3 times a day |
|---|---|
| ก่อน/หลัง อาหาร<br>gò:n/lang/aa-häan | before/after a meal |
| กินพร้อมอาหาร<br>gin prórm aa-häan | with a meal |

Health

# Doctor

........................................

| | |
|---|---|
| โรงพยาบาล<br>roong-pa-ya-baan | hospital |
| แผนกฉุกเฉิน<br>pà-nàek chùk-chürn | casualty department |
| ใบสั่งยา  bai-sàng-yaa | prescription |
| รถฉุกเฉิน<br>rót chùk-chürn | ambulance |

**FACE TO FACE**

**A** ฉันรู้สึกไม่สบาย
chan rúu sùk mâi sà baai
I don't feel right

**B** คุณมีไข้ไหม
khun mii kâi mái?
Do you have a temperature?

**A** ไม่มี/มี ฉันปวดตรงนี้
mâi mii/mii chan bpùat dtrong níi
No/Yes, I have a pain here

| I have broken... | ...ของฉันหัก |
| | ...kö:ng chan hàg |
| my foot | เท้าของฉัน |
| | táo kö:ng chan |
| my ankle | ข้อเท้าของฉัน |
| | kôr-táo kö:ng chan |
| my hand | มือของฉัน |
| | muu kö:ng chan |
| my arm | แขนของฉัน |
| | käen kö:ng chan |
| It hurts | มันเจ็บ |
| | man jèp |
| I need to see a doctor | ฉันต้องการไปหาหมอ |
| | chan dtô:ng gaan bpai häa mör |
| My son/daughter is ill | ลูกชาย/ลูกสาวของฉันไม่สบาย |
| | lûuk chaai/lûuk säao kö:ng chan mâi sà baai |
| Will he/she have to go to hospital? | ต้องไปโรงพยาบาลไหม |
| | dtô:ng bpai roong-pa-ya-baan mái? |
| I'm on the pill | ฉันกำลังกินยาประจำ |
| | chan gamlang gin yaa bprà jam |
| I'm diabetic | ฉันเป็นเบาหวาน |
| | chan bpen bao wäan |

| I need insulin | ฉันต้องการอินซูลิน |
| | chan dtô:ng gaan in-suu-lin |
| I'm allergic to penicillin | ฉันแพ้ยาเพนนิซิลิน |
| | chan páe yaa pen-ni-si-lin |
| Will I have to pay? | ฉันต้องจ่ายไหม |
| | chan dtô:ng jàai mái? |
| Can you give me a receipt for the insurance? | ขอใบเสร็จสำหรับไปเคลิ้ม ประกันด้วยครับ/ค่ะ |
| | kör bai-sèt säm-ràp bpai claim bpra-gan dûoy krab/ká? |

## Dentist

· · · · · · · · · · · · · · · · · · · · · · · · · · · · · · · · · · · · · · · ·

You will have to pay for dental treatment at the time of service. Ask for a receipt if you want to claim money back from your insurance company.

| อุดฟัน ùt fan | filling |
|---|---|
| ครอบฟัน krôrb fan | crown |
| ฟันปลอม fan bplorm | dentures |
| ฉีดยา chìid yaa | injection |

113

| I need to go to a dentist | ฉันต้องไปหาหมอฟัน |
| | chan dtô:ng bpai häa mör fan |
| He/she has toothache | เขา/เธอ ปวดฟัน |
| | käo/tur bpùat fan |
| This hurts | มันปวด |
| | man bpùat |
| My filling has come out | ที่อุดฟันหลุด |
| | tïi ùt fan lùt |
| My crown has come out | ที่ครอบฟันหลุด |
| | tïi krôrb fan lùt |
| Can you do emergency treatment? | คุณจะสามารถรักษาได้เลยหรือเปล่า |
| | khun jà säa-mâat rák-säa dâai leei rüu bplàao? |

# Different types of travellers

## Disabled travellers

. . . . . . . . . . . . . . . . . . . . . . . . . . . . . . . .

| | |
|---|---|
| Is there a toilet for the disabled? | มีห้องสุขาสำหรับคนพิการไหม<br>mii hô:ng su-käa säm-ràp kon pi-gaan mái? |
| I want a room on the ground floor | ฉันต้องการห้องชั้นล่าง<br>chan dtô:ng gaan hô:ng chán lâang |
| Can I visit in a wheelchair? | ฉันจะนั่งรถเข็นไปได้ไหม<br>chan jà nâng rót-kën bpai dâai mái? |
| Is there a lift? | ลิฟท์อยู่ที่ไหน<br>lift yùu tîi näi? |
| Is there a reduction for the disabled? | มีส่วนลดให้คนพิการไหม<br>mii sùan lód hâi kon pi-gaan mái? |
| I am deaf | ฉันเป็นคนหูหนวก<br>chan bpen kon hüu nùak |

> **Hotel (booking)** (p 56) > **Hotel desk** (p 59) 115

# With kids

| | |
|---|---|
| A child's ticket | ตั๋วเด็ก |
| | dtüa dèk |
| He/she is ... years old | เขา/เธอ อายุ ... ปี |
| | käo/tur aa-yú ... bpii |
| Is there a reduction for children? | มีส่วนลดสำหรับเด็กไหม |
| | mii sùan lód säm-ràp dèk mái? |
| Do you have a children's menu? | มีรายการอาหารสำหรับเด็กไหม |
| | mii raai-gaan aa-häan säm-ràp dèk mái? |
| Is it OK to take children? | พาเด็กไปด้วยได้ไหม |
| | paa dèk bpai dûoy dâai mái? |
| Do you have...? | คุณมี ... ไหม |
| | khun mii ... mái? |
| a high chair | โต๊ะสำหรับเด็ก |
| | dtó säm-ràp dèk |
| a cot | เปล/เตียงสำหรับเด็ก |
| | bplee/dtiang säm-ràp dèk |

# Reference

## Alphabet

........................................

Thai has 44 consonants and 32 vowel characters.
However, there are only 20 consonant sounds.
Below are the consonants which are pronounced in
the same way as in English.

| | |
|---|---|
| ก | = **g** as in **g**ood |
| ข ค ฆ | = **k** as in **k**ing |
| จ | = **j** as in **J**anuary |
| ซ ส, ษ, ศ | = **s** as in **s**eek |
| ด, ฎ | = **d** as in **d**oor |
| บ | = **b** as in **b**aby |
| ม | = **m** as in **m**other |
| น ณ | = **n** as in **n**oun |
| ล ฬ | = **l** as in **l**ove |
| ร | = **r** as in **r**oll |
| ว | = **w** as in **w**oman |
| ท ธ | = **t** as in **t**ime |
| ย, ญ | = **y** as in **y**ou |

พ = **f** as in **f**un
ห ฮ = **h** as in **h**oney

The following are a few sounds that are difficult to pronounce.

ฏ ต = **dt** as in s**t**op
ป = **bp** as in s**p**ain
ช ฌ ฉ = **ch** as in **ch**ange
ง = **ng** as in ri**ng**ing

Only 30 of the 32 vowels found in the Thai language are in use. They can be classified in two groups: short vowels and long vowels. The words in this book use a single letter or a single letter followed by a colon for short vowels, and a double letter or a combination of two letters for long vowels ('a' for a short vowel, and 'aa' for a long vowel).

# Measurements and quantities

• • • • • • • • • • • • • • • • • • • • • • • • • • • •

1 lb = approx. 0.5 kilo – 1 pint = approx. 0.5 litre

## Liquids

| | | |
|---|---|---|
| 1/2 litre of... | ...ครึ่งลิตร | krûng lít |
| one litre of... | ...หนึ่งลิตร | nùng lít |
| two litres of... | ...สองลิตร | sö:ng lít |
| a bottle of... | ...หนึ่งขวด | nùng kùat |
| a glass of... | ...หนึ่งแก้ว | nùng gâew |

## Weights

| | | |
|---|---|---|
| 100 grams of... | ...หนึ่งขีด | nùng kìit |
| 1/2 kilo of... | ...ครึ่งกิโล | krûng gi-loo |
| one kilo of... | ...หนึ่งกิโล | nùng gi-loo |
| two kilos of... | ...สองกิโล | sö:ng gi-loo |

## Food

| a slice of... | ...หนึ่งชิ้น | ...nùng chín |
| a dozen | ...หนึ่งโหล | ...nùng-lŏo |
| a box of... | ...หนึ่งกล่อง | ...nùng glò:ng |
| a carton of... | ...หนึ่งคัทตอน | ...nùng cut-tô:n |

## Miscellaneous

| double | สองเท่า | sö:ng tâo |
| more | มาก | mâak |
| less | น้อย | nói |
| enough | เพียงพอ | piang-por |
| single | อันเดียว | an-diao |

# Numbers

In the Thai language, the noun doesn't change when it becomes a plural noun. For example, in English you would say 'two eggs', but in Thai you say 'two egg'. In Thai numbers, there are many classifiers used for objects and people. A classifier is a group to which something belongs – a category. For instance, a cat might be classified as an animal, a carrot as a vegetable, or a house as a building. If you are not sure which classifier to use, you can use the word 'an/อัน' (thing) with most of the objects.

| 0 | ศูนย์ | sŭun |
| 1 | หนึ่ง | nùng |
| 2 | สอง | sŏ:ng |
| 3 | สาม | săam |
| 4 | สี่ | sìi |
| 5 | ห้า | hâa |
| 6 | หก | hòk |
| 7 | เจ็ด | jèt |
| 8 | แปด | bpàet |
| 9 | เก้า | gâao |
| 10 | สิบ | sìp |
| 11 | สิบเอ็ด | sìp-èt |
| 12 | สิบสอง | sìp-sŏ:ng |
| 13 | สิบสาม | sìp-săam |
| 14 | สิบสี่ | sìp-sìi |
| 15 | สิบห้า | sìp hâa |

Numbers

| 16 | สิบหก | sìp hòk |
| 17 | สิบเจ็ด | sìp jèt |
| 18 | สิบแปด | sìp bpàet |
| 19 | สิบเก้า | sìp gâao |
| 20 | ยี่สิบ | yîi sìp |
| 30 | สามสิบ | săam-sìp |
| 40 | สี่สิบ | sìi sìp |
| 50 | ห้าสิบ | hâa-sìp |
| 60 | หกสิบ | hòk-sìp |
| 70 | เจ็ดสิบ | jèt-sìp |
| 80 | แปดสิบ | bpàet-sìp |
| 90 | เก้าสิบ | gâao-sìp |
| 100 | หนึ่งร้อย | nùng-ró:i |
| 200 | สองร้อย | sö:ng-ró:i |
| 300 | สามร้อย | săam-ró:i |
| 400 | สี่ร้อย | sìi-ró:i |
| 500 | ห้าร้อย | hâa-ró:i |
| 1000 | หนึ่งพัน | nùng-pan |
| 2000 | สองพัน | sö:ng-pan |
| 3000 | สามพัน | săam-pan |
| 10,000 | หนึ่งหมื่น | nùng-mùun |

| 100,000 | หนึ่งแสน | nùng-săen |
| 1,000,000 | หนึ่งล้าน | nùng-láan |

| | | | | |
|---|---|---|---|---|
| 1st | อันดับหนึ่ง<br>an-dàp-nùng | 6th | อันดับหก<br>an-dàp-hòk |
| 2nd | อันดับสอง<br>an-dàp-sŏ:ng | 7th | อันดับเจ็ด<br>an-dàp-jèt |
| 3rd | อันดับสาม<br>an-dàp-săam | 8th | อันดับแปด<br>an-dàp-bpàet |
| 4th | อันดับสี่<br>an-dàp-sìi | 9th | อันดับเก้า<br>an-dàp-gâao |
| 5th | อันดับห้า<br>an-dàp-hâa | 10th | อันดับสิบ<br>an-dàp-sìp |

# Days and months

## Days วัน wan

| Monday | วันจันทร์ | wan-jan |
| Tuesday | วันอังคาร | wan-ang-kaan |
| Wednesday | วันพุธ | wan-pút |
| Thursday | วันพฤหัสบดี | wan-pá-rú-hàt-<br>sa-bo:-dii |

| Friday | วันศุกร์ | wan-sùk |
| Saturday | วันเสาร์ | wan-säo |
| Sunday | วันอาทิตย์ | wan-aa-tít |
| Weekend | วันหยุด เสาร์อาทิตย์ | wan yùt säo- aa-tít |

## Months เดือน duan

| January | มกราคม | má-gà-raa-kom |
| February | กุมภาพันธ์ | gum-paa-pan |
| March | มีนาคม | mii-naa-kom |
| April | เมษายน | mee-säa-yon |
| May | พฤษภาคม | prút-sa-paa-kom |
| June | มิถุนายน | mí-tù-naa-yon |
| July | กรกฎาคม | gà-rá-gà-daa-kom |
| August | สิงหาคม | sing-häa-kom |
| September | กันยายน | gan-yaa-yon |
| October | ตุลาคม | dtù-laa-kom |
| November | พฤศจิกายน | prút-sà-jí-gaa-yon |
| December | ธันวาคม | tan-waa-kom |

## Seasons

หน้าร้อน   nâa rórn   **Hot season** (hot and humid;
   March to June)

หน้าฝน   nâa fön   **Rainy season** (heavy rainfall,
   not a good time to visit; July to October)

หน้าหนาว   nâa näao   **Cool season** (cool in the
   morning and at night, the best time to visit;
   November to February)

## Time

The 24-hour clock is used in timetables, etc.

| ตอนเช้า<br>dtorn cháao | a.m. (morning) |
|---|---|
| ตอนเที่ยงวัน<br>dtorn tîang wan | It's midday |
| ตอนบ่าย<br>dtorn bàai | p.m. (afternoon) |

| It's... | มันเป็นเวลา... |
| | man bpen wee-laa... |
| It's 1 o'clock (afternoon) | มันเป็นเวลาบ่ายหนึ่ง |
| | man bpen wee-laa bàai nùng |
| It's 2 o'clock (afternoon) | มันเป็นเวลาบ่ายสอง |
| | man bpen wee-laa bàai sö:ng |
| What time is it? | กี่โมงแล้ว |
| | gìi moong láew? |
| 9.00 | เก้าโมงตรง |
| | gâao moong dtrong |
| 9.10 | เก้าโมงสิบนาที |
| | gâao moong sìp naa-tii |
| 9.15 | เก้าโมงสิบห้านาที |
| | gâao moong sìp hâa naa-tii |
| 9.30 | เก้าโมงสามสิบนาที |
| | gâao moong säam sìp naa-tii |
| 9.45 | เก้าโมงสี่สิบห้านาที |
| | gâao moong sìi sìp hâa naa-tii |
| 9.50 | เก้าโมงห้าสิบนาที |
| | gâao moong hâa sìp naa-tii |
| What is the date? | วันนี้วันที่อะไร |
| | wan níi wan-tîi a-rai? |

| It's 16 September 2006 | วันที่ 16 กันยายน 2006 |
| | wan-tîi sìp hòk gan-yaa-yon sö:ng pan hòk |
| today | วันนี้ |
| | wan níi |
| tomorrow | พรุ่งนี้ |
| | prûng níi |
| yesterday | เมื่อวานนี้ |
| | mûa waan níi |

## Time phrases

| When does it begin/finish? | เมื่อไหร่มันจะเริ่ม/เสร็จ |
| | mûa-rài man jà rûrm/sèt? |
| When does it open/close? | เมื่อไหร่มันจะเปิด/ปิด |
| | mûa-rài man jà bpùrd/bpìd? |
| When does it leave? | มันจะออกเมื่อไหร่ |
| | man jà òrk mûa-rài? |
| When does it return? | มันจะกลับเมื่อไหร่ |
| | man jà glàb mûa-rài? |
| at 3 o'clock (afternoon) | บ่ายสาม |
| | bàai säam |

| before 3 o'clock (afternoon) | ก่อนบ่ายสาม |
| | gò:n bàai säam |
| after 3 o'clock (afternoon) | หลังบ่ายสาม |
| | läng bàai säam |
| in the morning | ตอนเช้า |
| | dto:n cháao |
| this morning | เช้านี้ |
| | cháao níi |
| in the afternoon (until dusk) | บ่ายนี้ |
| | bàai níi |
| in the evening (after dusk) | ตอนเย็น |
| | dto:n yen |
| in an hour's time | ภายในหนึ่งชั่วโมง |
| | paai-nai nùng chûa moong |

# Eating out

## Eating places

A wide variety of food is available at all times of the day and night in Thailand, from fresh fruits to three course dinners. You can choose to eat in restaurants, the food courts in the shopping centres or at street shops. At street shops you sit down and eat right by the side of the road (be sure to drink bottled water and not the tap water from these shops).

| ESTABLISHMENTS | TYPE OF FOOD SERVED |
|---|---|
| ร้านอาหารตามสั่ง<br>ráan aa-häan-dtaam-sàng | fried rice and fried noodles |
| ร้านก๋วยเตี๋ยว<br>ráan güai-dtïao | non-stir-fried noodles with soup or without soup |

| | |
|---|---|
| ร้านข้าวมันไก่<br>ráan kâao-man-gài | steamed rice cooked with chicken soup, and served with boiled chicken |
| ร้านข้าวหมูแดง<br>ráan kâao müu-daeng | rice topped with barbecued pork |
| ร้านข้าวหน้าเป็ด<br>ráan kâao nâa-bpèt | rice topped with barbecued duck |
| ร้านข้าวขาหมู<br>ráan kâao käa- müu | rice with stewed pork |
| ร้านอาหารซีฟู้ด<br>ráan aa-häan-sea-food | seafood |
| ร้านผัดไทย<br>ráan pàt-tai | traditional Thai noodles |
| คาเฟ่<br>kà-fé | variety of foods and alcohol and feature live music |
| ร้านกาแฟ<br>ràan gaa- fae | hot tea and coffee, iced tea and coffee, and other soft drinks |

| | |
|---|---|
| ภัตตาคาร<br>pat-dtaa-kaan | variety of foods, they offer a higher standard of service than other establishments |
| ผับ/ในท์คลับ<br>pub/night-club | variety of foods and alcohol and feature live music |
| คาราโอเกะ<br>kaa-raa-o-gè | variety of foods and alcohol and feature karaoke |
| ร้านไอศครีม<br>ràan ai-sa-kriim | ice cream |
| ร้านข้าวต้ม<br>ràan kâao dtôm | rice soup |
| ร้านโจ๊ก<br>ràan jók | porridge rice (for breakfast) |
| ร้านยำ<br>ràan yam | Thai salads |

# In a bar/café

Since Thailand is a hot country, hot drinks are not popular. However, you can find teas and coffees in hotel lobbies and some quality restaurants. Don't forget to try Thai iced coffee, Thai herbal drinks and Thai fruit juices such as guava nectar juice and coconut juice. The selling of alcohol is prohibited on Buddhist holy days, the King's birthday and the Queen's birthday.

| | |
|---|---|
| What would you like? | คุณต้องการดื่มอะไร |
| | khun dtô:ng gaan dùum a-rai? |
| Hot coffee/hot tea please | กาแฟร้อน/ชาร้อน ครับ/ค่ะ |
| | gaa-fae ró:n/ chaa ró:n krab/kà |
| A ... please | ...หนึ่งแก้ว |
| | ...nùng gâew |
| 2 ... please | ...สองแก้ว |
| | ...sö:ng gàew |
| 3 ... please | ...สามแก้ว |
| | ...säam gàew |
| Do you have...? | คุณมี ... ไหม |
| | khun miiee ... mái? |

| | |
|---|---|
| Do you have beer? | คุณมีเบียร์ไหม |
| | khun mii beer mái? |
| Do you have brandy? | คุณมีบรั่นดีไหม |
| | khun mii brandy mái? |
| a bottle of sparkling water | ขอโซดาขวดหนึ่ง |
| | kör sò-daa kùat nùng |
| sparkling mineral water | โซดา |
| | sò-daa |
| still mineral water | น้ำแร่ |
| | náam-râe |
| A cappuccino, please | ขอคาปูชิโน่ หนึ่งแก้ว ครับ/คะ |
| | kör ka-bpuu-chi-nôo nùng gâew krab/kà |
| A tea, please | ขอชาร้อนหนึ่งที่ครับ/ค่ะ |
| | kör chaa- ró:n nùng tîi krab/kà |
| with milk | ชาใส่นม |
| | chaa-sài-nom |
| with lemon | ชามะนาว |
| | chaa-ma-naow |
| with ice | ชาดำเย็น |
| | chaa-dam-yen |
| with sugar | ใส่น้ำตาลด้วย |
| | sài náam dtaan dûoy |

133

| without sugar | ไม่ใส่น้ำตาล |
| | mài sài náam dtaan |
| one more, please | ใส่น้ำตาลอีกหน่อยครับ/ |
| | ค่ะ |
| | sài náam dtaan ìik nòi krab/kà |

# Reading the menu

When eating in a restaurant, you may start with some appetizers such as deep-fried shrimps กุ้งทอด gûng tôrt, **spring rolls** ปอเปี๊ยะ bpo:-bpía, **deep-fried squid** ปลาหมึกชุบแป้งทอด bplaa-mùk chúp bpâeng tôrt, **chicken sàtée** ไก่สะเต๊ะ gài sà-dté, **Thai salad** ยำ yams, etc.

Usually soup is served with the main course. A cup of sweet dessert or some fruits follow the main course. Breads are not usually served with Thai food. Order your food in the order in which you want each dish to be served. Some restaurants may add a service charge of about 10–15% to your bill, so be sure to check before leaving tips.

| | |
|---|---|
| **menu** | รายการอาหาร  raai gaan aa-hăan |
| appetizers | อาหารว่าง  aa-hăan wâang |
| Thai salad | ยำ  yam |
| fried rice | ข้าวผัด  kâao-pàd |
| stir-fry | ผัด  pàd |
| soup | น้ำแกง  náam-gaeng |
| curry | แกง  gaeng |
| chili sauce | น้ำพริก  náam- prík |
| dessert | ของหวาน  kö:ng- wăan |

## In a restaurant

• • • • • • • • • • • • • • • • • • • • • • • • • • • • • • • •

| | |
|---|---|
| The menu, please | ขอเมนูด้วยครับ/ค่ะ |
| | kör menu dûoy krab/ká |
| Is there a set menu? | มีเมนูชุดไหม |
| | mii menu chút mái? |
| What is this? | นี่คืออะไร |
| | nîi kuu a-rai? |

135

| I'd like this | ฉันต้องการอันนี้ |
| | chan dtô:ng gaan an níi |
| What is the speciality of the house? | อะไรที่อร่อยของร้านนี้ |
| | a-rai tîi aròːy kŏːng ráan níi? |
| Excuse me! | ขอโทษนะครับ/คะ |
| | kŏr tôot ná krab/ká! |
| The bill, please | เก็บเงินด้วยครับ/ค่ะ |
| | gèb ngurn dûoy krab/ká |
| Some more rice/ water, please | ขอข้าว/น้ำ เพิ่มด้วยครับ/ คะ |
| | kŏr kâao/náam pûrm dûoy krab/ká |
| salt | เกลือ |
| | glua |
| pepper | พริกไทย |
| | prík-tai |
| Another bottle, please | ขออันนี้อีกขวด |
| | kŏr an níi ìik kùat |
| Another glass, please | ขออันนี้อีกแก้ว |
| | kŏr an níi ìik gâew |

# Vegetarian

•••••••••••••••••••••••••••••••••••

Some restaurants sell vegetarian food all year round,
but you will find more vegetarian food available
during mid-October when the vegetarian festival
เทศกาลกินเจ   teet-sà-gaan gin-jee   takes place.

| | |
|---|---|
| I am vegetarian | ฉันเป็นมังสวิรัต |
| | chan bpen mang sà-vi-rát |
| I don't eat meat | ฉันไม่กินเนื้อสัตว์ |
| | chan mâi gin núa-sàt |
| Is there meat in this? | มีเนื้อสัตว์ในอาหารนี้หรือเปล่า |
| | mii núa-sàt nai aa-häan níi rüü bplàao? |
| What is there without meat? | มีอาหารอะไรบ้างที่ไม่มีเนื้อสัตว์ |
| | mii aa-häan a-rai bâang tîi mâi mii núa-sàt? |

## Vegetarian dishes

ผัดไทยเจ pàd-tai-jee stir-fried Thai noodles with
bean sprouts, tofu and crushed peanut

ผัดพริกมะเขือยาว pàd-prík-ma-kŭa-yaow
stir-fried aubergine with red chilli, pepper and basil
leaves

ต้มยำเห็ด dtôm-yam-hèt hot and sour
mushroom soup

ข้าวผัดผักรวมมิตร kâao-pàd-pàk-ruam-mit
fried rice with various vegetables

ข้าวผัดเผือก kâao-pàd-pùak fried rice with taro

แกงเขียวหวานเจ gaeng-kǐao-wǎan-jee green
curry with various vegetables

แกงเผ็ดเจ gaeng-pèt-jee red curry with various
vegetables

จับฉ่าย jàb-chàai steamed mixed vegetables

ผัดผักรวมมิตร pàd-pàk-ruam-mit stir-fried
various vegetables

ผัดซีอิ๊วเจ pàd-sii-íao-jee stir-fried noodles with
black soya-sauce

ก๋วยเตี๋ยวเจ gŭai-dtĭao-jee stir-fried noodles with
various vegetables and tofu

เต้าหู้ทอด dtâo-hûu-tôrt deep-fried tofu served
with sweet peanut sauce

เผือกทอด pùak-tôrt deep-fried taro served with
sweet peanut sauce

ปอเปี๊ยะทอด bpo:-bpía-tôrt deep-fried spring roll
served with plum sauce

# Wines and spirits

Some Thai beers are very popular with tourists, and
Thai wines are also available at local restaurants,
nightclubs, pubs, etc.

| | |
|---|---|
| The wine list, please | ขอรายการไวน์ด้วยครับ / คะ |
| | kör raai-gaan wine dûoy krab/ká |
| Can you recommend a good wine? | คุณจะแนะนำไวน์ดีดี ได้ไหม |
| | khun jà náe-nam wine dii dii dâai mái? |
| A bottle of... | ...หนึ่งขวด |
| | ...nùng kùat |

139

| red/white wine | ไวน์แดง/ไวน์ขาว |
| | wine-daeng/wine-käao |
| A glass of... | ...หนึ่งแก้ว |
| | ...nùng gâew |
| a dry wine | ไวน์แห้ง |
| | wine-hâeng |
| a local wine | ไวน์พื้นเมือง |
| | wine-púun-muang |
| a sweet wine | ไวน์หวาน |
| | wine-wäan |

# Common dishes

Appetizers อาหารว่าง aa-häan wâang

ขนมจีบ kä-nöm-jìip steamed wonton
   (pork/shrimp)

ขนมปังหน้าหมู kä-nöm- bpang-nâa- müu deep-
   fried bread top with pork

เกี๊ยวกุ้ง gíao gûng deep-fried shrimp wonton

ทอดมันปลากราย tôrt-man- bplaa kraai fish
   cake

ทอดมันกุ้ง tôrt-man-gûng  shrimp cake

หมูสะเต๊ะ müu-sà-dtê  barbecued pork served
  with peanut curry sauce

หมูย่าง müu-yâang  barbecued pork

ปอเปี๊ยะ bpo:-bpía  deep-fried spring roll (pork)

ปลาหมึกชุบแป้งทอด bplaa mùk chúp bpâeng tôrt
  deep-fried squid

กุ้งชุบแป้งทอด gûng chúp bpâeng tôrt  deep-fried
  shrimps

เต้าหู้ทอด dtâo-hûu-tôrt  deep-fried tofu

ปีกไก่ทอด bpìik gái-tôrt  deep-fried chicken wings

## Salad ยำ yam

ส้มตำ sôm dtam  papaya salad (spicy and sour)

ยำถั่วพู yam tùa puu  winged bean salad (sweet
  and sour)

ยำสามกรอบ yam säam grorb  crispy squid,
  shrimp and cashew nuts salad, (spicy and sour)

ยำทะเล yam tà-lee  seafood salad (spicy and sour)

ยำปูอัด yam bpuu àt  crab salad (spicy and sour)

ยำใส้กรอก yam sâi gròrk  pork sausage salad
  (spicy and sour)

ย่าหมูยอ yam müu yor  Thai pork sausage salad
(spicy and sour)

ย่าวุ้นเส้น yam wún sên  glass noodle salad (spicy
and sour)

สลัด sà-làd  vegetable salad

สลัดแขก sà-làd kèek  vegetable salad with peanut
dressing

สลัดทะเล sà-làd tà-lee  seafood salad (not spicy)

## Soup น้ำแกง náam-gaeng

ต้มย่ำ dtôm yam  delicious savoury soup with
shrimps, mushrooms, lemongrass, and Thai chilli

แกงจืดเต้าหู้ทรงเครื่อง gaeng jùut dtâo-hûu
song krûang  tofu soup

แกงจืดสาหร่ายทะเล gaeng jùut säa-ràai tà-lee
seaweed soup

ต้มซุปไก่ dtôm soup gài  chicken soup with mixed
vegetables

## Meat เนื้อ núa

เนื้อวัว núa-wua **beef**
เนื้อไก่ núa gài **chicken**
เนื้อหมู núa müu **pork**
เนื้อเป็ด núa bpèt **duck**

## Fish and seafood ปลาและอาหารทะเล
bplaa láe aa-häan ta-lee

กุ้งมังกร gûng mang gorn **lobster**
ปลาหมึก bplaa mùk **squid**
กุ้ง gûng **prawns**
หอย höːi **mussels**
ปลาดุก bplaa dùk **catfish**
ปลาช่อน bplaa chôːn **serpenthead**
ปู bpuu **crab**
ปลาน้ำจืด bplaa náam jùut **freshwater fish**
ปลาทะเล bplaa tà-lee **saltwater fish**

# Desserts ของหวาน kö:ng wǎan

กล้วยบวชชี glûai bùat-chii  Thai bananas cooked with coconut milk

ฝอยทอง fö:i-torng  egg yolk poured into hot syrup

เค้กนมสด cake nom sòt  fresh milk cake

ลูกบัวถั่วแดงเย็น lûuk-bua tùa daeng yen  sweet red bean and lotus tip in syrup

พายมะพร้าว paai mà-práao  coconut pie

# Menu reader

ก

เกี๊ยวกุ้ง gíao gûng  wonton shrimps

เกี๊ยวซ่า gíao sâa  fried wonton (pork)

แกงเขียวหวาน gaeng kĭao-wăan  green curry
  (with chicken, beef or shrimps)

แกงเผ็ด gaeng pèt  red curry

แกงเผ็ดเป็ดย่าง gaeng pèt bpèt yâang  roast duck
  curry with cherry tomatoes

แกงเลียง gaeng liang  hot vegetable consommé
  with prawns

แกงจืดเต้าหู้ gaeng jùut dtâo-hûu  tofu soup

แกงป่าลูกชิ้นปลากราย gaeng bpàa lûuk chín
  bplaa kraai  jungle curry with fish balls

แกงมัสมั่น gaeng mat-sà-màn mat-sà-màn  curry
  (yellow curry) with chicken/beef

แกงส้ม gaeng sôm  hot and sour tamarind soup
  with fish

ไก่ผัดพริก gài pàt prík  chicken with Thai chilli

ไก่ผัดพริกขิง gài pàt prík king **chicken with string beans in dry red curry**

ไก่ย่าง gài yâang **barbecued chicken**

ไก่ห่อใบเตย gài hòr bai dteei **chicken nuggets wrapped in Toey leaves (pandon leaves)**

ไก่อบน้ำแดง gài òp náam daeng **steamed chicken in a clay pot**

ไก่อบน้ำผึ้ง gài òp náam pûng **steamed chicken with honey**

กะหล่ำปลี gà-làm-bplii **cabbage**

กาแฟ gaa-fae **coffee**

กาแฟเย็น gaa-fae yen **iced coffee**

กาแฟสำเร็จรูป gaa-fae säm-rèt- rûub **instant coffee**

กุ้งเผา gûng päo **barbecued shrimps**

กุ้งแช่น้ำปลา gûng châe náam bplaa **raw shrimps in fish sauce and Thai chilli**

กุ้งชุบแป้งทอด gûng chúp bpâeng tôrt **deep-fried shrimps**

กุ้งมังกร gûng mang gorn **lobster**

กุ้งอบวุ้นเส้น gûng òp wún sên **steamed shrimps and glass noodles in a clay pot**

ข

ไข่ต้ม kài dtôm  boiled eggs

เข้มข้น kêm-kôn  strong taste

ข้าว kâao  steamed rice

ข้าวเหนียว kâao-nïao  steamed sticky rice

ข้าวเหนียวหมูย่าง kâao-nïao müu yâang
  steamed sticky rice with barbecued pork

ข้าวคลุกกะปิ kâao klúg gà-pi  shrimp paste fried
  rice with condiments

ข้าวต้ม kâao dtôm  rice soup

ข้าวผัดปู kâao pàt bpuu  crab fried rice

ข้าวอบสับปะรด kâao òp sàp-bpa-rót  pineapple
  fried rice

ค

คะน้าผัดน้ำมันหอย kà-náa pàt náam man hö:i
  stir-fried Chinese kale with oyster sauce

คะน้าผัดปลาเค็ม kà-náa pàt bplaa kem  stir-fried
  Chinese kale with salty fish

ง

เงาะ ngó:  rambutan

จ

จับฉ่าย jàb-chàai steamed mixed vegetables with pork or chicken

โจ๊ก jók porridge rice

ช

ชาดำเย็น chaa dam yen iced tea

ชามะนาว cha ma-naow lemon tea

ชาสมุนไพร chaa sa-mŭn-prai herb tea

ซ

ซาลาเปา sà-la-bpao Chinese bun

ซี่โครงหมูสามรส sîi-kroong mŭu săam rót sweet and sour pork ribs

ซี่โครงหมูย่าง sîi-kroong-mŭu-yâang barbecued pork ribs

ซีอิ๊วขาว sii-íu-kăao soy bean sauce

ซุปเห็ด soup hèt mushroom soup

ซุปมะเขือเทศ soup má-kŭa-têet tomato soup

ซุปหน่อไม้ soup nòr màai young bamboo shoot salad (spicy)

แซนวิชทูน่า sand-wit-tuu-nâa tuna sandwich

ด

แตงโม dtaeng-moo watermelon

148

แตงกวา dtaeng-gwaa  cucumber

ต้มข่าไก่ dtôm kàa gài  lemongrass soup with
  coconut milk and chicken

ต้มยำกุ้ง dtôm yam gûng  spicy lemongrass soup
  with river prawns

ตำส้มโอ dtam sôm-oo  spicy pomelo salad

ท

ทอดมันกุ้ง tôrt man gûng  shrimp cake

ทอดมันปลากราย tôrt man bplaa kraai  fish cake

ทับทิม táb-tim  pomegranate

ทุเรียน tú-rian  durian

น

เนื้อแดดเดียว núa dàet diao  deep-fried beef

เนื้อตุ๋น núa dtün  steamed beef

น

น้อยหน่า nó:i nàa  **custard apple**

น้ำแกง náam gaeng  soup

น้ำแข็ง náam käeng  ice

น้ำแข็งเปล่า náam käeng bplàao  ice with water

น้ำแร่ náam râe  mineral water

น้ำแอ๊ปเปิ้ล náam apple  apple juice

น้ำดื่ม náam dùum  drinking water

น้ำตาล náam dtaan  sugar

น้ำตาลสด náam dtaan sòt  sugar palm sap

น้ำปลา náam bplaa  fish sauce

น้ำผลไม้ náam pönla-máai  fruit juice

น้ำผึ้ง náam-pûng  honey

น้ำฝรั่ง náam fa-ràng  guava juice

น้ำพริกกะปิ náam prík gà pi  shrimp paste dip
  served with deep-fried mackerel

น้ำพริกหนุ่ม náam prík nùm  northern spicy dips
  served with assorted vegetables

น้ำมะเขือเทศ náam má-küa-têet  tomato juice

น้ำมะนาว náam ma-naow  lime juice

น้ำมะพร้าวอ่อน náam mà-práao òrn  coconut
  juice

น้ำมะม่วง náam má-mûang  mango juice

น้ำมันมะกอก náam man mà-gò:k  olive oil

น้ำลำไย náam lam yai  longan juice

น้ำลิ้นจี่ náam lín jìi  lychee juice

น้ำส้มสายชู náam sôm säai chuu  vinegar

น้ำสับปะรด náam sàp-bpa-rót  pineapple juice

น้ำองุ่น náam a-ngùn  grape juice

บ

เบียร์ beer **beer**

บรั่นดี brandy **brandy**

บะหมี่เกี๊ยว bà mìi gíao **egg noodle soup with wontons**

บะหมี่หมูแดง bà mìi müu daeng **egg noodle soup with barbecued pork**

ป

ปลา bplaa **fish**

ปลาเก๋าราดพริก bplaa käo râat prík **grouper fish with chilli, garlic and pepper (sweet and sour sauce)**

ปลากะพงทอดกรอบ bplaa gà pong tôrt krorb **deep-fried sea bass**

ปลากะพงนึ่งมะนาว bplaa gà pong nûng ma-naow **steamed sea bass with lime**

ปลากราย bplaa graai **chitala fish**

ปลาช่อน bplaa chô:n **Thai catfish**

ปาท่องโก๋ bpaa tô:ng-göo **Chinese doughnuts**

ปลาสำลีเผา bplaa säm-lii päo **grilled black banded trevally fish**

ปลาหมึก bplaa mùk **squid**

ปลาหมึกเผา bplaa mùk päo **grilled squid**

ปลาหมึกทอด bplaa mùk tôrt  deep-fried squid

ปูเผา bpuu päo  grilled crab

ปูจ๋า bpuu jä  steamed crab

ปูผัดผงกระหรี่ bpuu pàt pöng gà-rii  crab with egg
  and curry sauce/garlic and pepper

เป็ดตุ๋นน้ำใส bpèt dtün náam säi  steamed duck

เป็ดย่าง bpèt yâang  grilled duck

ผ

ผลไม้ pönla-máai  fruit

ผักกาดแก้ว pàk gàad-gâew  iceberg lettuce

ผัดเปรี้ยวหวาน pàt bpriao-wän  stir-fried
  vegetables with shrimps (sweet and sour)

ผัดเผ็ดปลาดุก pàt pèt bplaa dùk  deep-fried
  catfish topped with chilli sauce

ผัดเม็ดมะม่วงหิมพานต์ pàt mét má-mûang
  hïm mà paan  chicken stir-fried with cashew nuts
  and dried chilli

ผัดไทย pàt tai  Thai noodles

ผัดซี่อิ๊ว pàt sii-íu  fried rice noodles with soy sauce

ผัดถั่วงอกเต้าหู้หมูสับ pàt tùa ngô:k dtâo-hûu
  müu sàb  stir-fried tofu with bean sprouts

ผัดถั่วลันเตา pàt tùa lan-dtao  stir-fried snow
  peas with shrimp
ผัดผักรวมมิตร pàt pàk ruam mit  stir-fried
  vegetables
ผัดวุ้นเส้น pàt wún sên  stir-fried glass noodles
  with eggs
พ
แพนเค็ก paan-cake  pancake
แพนง pà-naeng  sweet curry with meat
พริกไทย prík tai  black pepper
พริกขี้หนู prík kîi nŭu  Thai chilli (very spicy)
พริกน้ำปลา prík náam bplaa  chilli in fish sauce
พริกป่น prík bpòn  crushed chilli
ภ
ภัดตาคาร pát-dtaa-kaan  restaurant
ย
แยม yaem  jam
แยม ผลไม้ yaem pönla-máai  fruit jam
ย่าถั่วพู yam tùa puu  spicy winged bean salad
ย่าปลาดุกฟู yam bplaa dùk fuu  deep-fried minced
  catfish with spicy mango salad

ยำปลาหมึก yam bplaa mùk  spicy squid salad

ยำผักกะเฉด yam pàk ga-chèet  spicy water
  mimosa salad

ยำวุ้นเส้น yam wún sên  spicy glass noodle salad
  with seafood

ส

เสต็ก steak  steak

สตรอเบอรี่ sa-dtror-bur-rii  strawberries

ส้ม sôm  orange

ส้มเขียวหวาน sôm kiao-wäan  sweet orange

ส้มโอ sôm-oo  pomelo

ส้มตำ sôm dtam  spicy papaya salad

สลัด sà-làd  salad

สลัดกุ้ง sà-làd gûng  shrimp salad

สับปะรด sàp-bpa-rót  pineapple

สุกี้ยากี้ suu-kîi-yaa-kîi  sukiyaki

ล

ลาบไก่ lâab gài  hot chicken salad

ลำไย lam-yai  longan

ลิ้นจี่ lín jìi  lychee

ว

วิสกี้ whisky  whisky

ห

หน่อไม้ nòr màai  young bamboo shoot

หน่อไม้ฝรั่งผัดใส่กุ้ง nòr màai fa-ràng pàt sài
  gûng  stir-fried asparagus with shrimps

หมี่กรอบ mìi kròrb  crispy sweet and sour rice
  noodles

หมูสะเต๊ะ mûu sa-dté  barbecued pork served with
  peanut curry sauce

หมูทอดกระเทียมพริกไทย mûu tôrt grà-tiam
  prík tai  pork with garlic and pepper

หอยแมงภู่อบหม้อดิน höːi maeng-pûu òp môr
  din  steamed mussels in a clay pot

หอยทอด höːi tôrt  crispy mussels

ห่อหมกทะเล hòr-mòk tà-lee  steamed seafood
  curry paté

อ

องุ่น a-ngùn  grapes

แอ็ปเปิ้ล apple  apple

ฮ

แฮม ham  ham

# Grammar

## Sentence structure

● ● ● ● ● ● ● ● ● ● ● ● ● ● ● ● ● ● ● ● ● ● ● ● ● ● ● ● ● ●

The basic Thai sentence structure is the same as in English: subject + verb + object. There is no gap to indicate separate syllables, words or sentences. Vowels are written above, below, before or after the consonant that they relate to.

## Pronouns

● ● ● ● ● ● ● ● ● ● ● ● ● ● ● ● ● ● ● ● ● ● ● ● ● ● ● ● ● ●

There is no difference in the form of pronouns in Thai when used as subject or object. However, there are many pronouns in the Thai language for the pronoun 'I/me'. The choice depends on the gender of the speaker.

| | | |
|---|---|---|
| I/me | ฉัน | chan<br>chan is used by both males and females when speaking to friends. |
| | ผม | pöm<br>pöm is used by males only.<br>pöm is a polite word to use. |
| | ดิฉัน | di-chan<br>di-chan is used by females only. Again, it is a polite word. |
| you | คุณ | khun |
| we/us | เรา | rao |
| he/him | เขา | käo |
| she/her | เธอ | tur |
| they/them | พวกเขา | puag-käo |
| it | มัน | man<br>man is a pronoun normally used for referring to animals – and everything other than humans. |
| children | หนู | nüu |

# Verbs

Verbs are not modified for different tenses, plurals
or gender. There is no article such as 'a', 'an' or 'the'.
The Thai language uses either the context or adverbs
of time to indicate the period of time of an activity.
The following are the common words used to
indicate tenses.

## Present continuous tense

กำลัง  gamlang = verb 'to be' + verb(ing).
For example:

I am going to Pattayaa.  ผมกำลังไปพัทยา
  pöm gamlang bpai pattaya

## Future tense

**ja**  ja + verb + period of time (not required).
For example:

I will go to Pattaya next week
  ผมจะไปพัทยาอาทิตย์หน้า  pöm ja bpai
  pattaya aa-tíd nâa

## Past tense

It is very simple to form the past tense in Thai. You add the period of time to indicate the past. For example:

I went to Pattaya yesterday

ผมไปพัทยาเมื่อวานนี้  pöm bpai pattaya mûa waan níi

# Adjectives

In the English language, adjectives are usually placed in front of the nouns they modify. In the Thai language, on the other hand, adjectives come after the nouns they describe. For example:

Chiang Mai is a beautiful city

เชียงใหม่เป็นเมืองสวย  chiang mai bpen muangng süay

# Negatives

•••••••••••••••••••••••••••••••••••••••••••••

The word ไม่ mâi is used in a negative sentence.
We place the word ไม่ mâi in front of the verb in
the sentence. For example:

I am hungry ฉัน หิว ข้าว  chan hïu kâao

I am not hungry ฉัน ไม่ หิว ข้าว  chang mâi hïu
kâao

He likes spicy food เขาชอบอาหารเผ็ด
käo chô:p aa-häan pèt

He does not like spicy food
เขาไม่ชอบอาหารเผ็ด käo mâi chô:p aa-häan
pèt

She wants to go shopping เธออยากไปซื้อของ
turr yàak bpai súu kö:ng

She doesn't want to go shopping
เธอไม่อยากไปซื้อของ tur mâi yàak bpai súu
kö:ng

# Questions

. . . . . . . . . . . . . . . . . . . . . . . . . . . . . . . . . . . . . .

Unlike in the English language, in Thai the question words are placed at the end of the sentence. The structure is subject + verb + object + question word. There is no need to put a question mark at the end of the sentence. The following are useful Thai question words:

| | | |
|---|---|---|
| what | อะไร | a-rai |
| when | เมื่อไหร่ | mûa-rài |
| where | ที่ไหน | tîi näi |
| why | ทำไม | tam-mai |
| how | อย่างไร | yàang-rai |
| who/whom | ใคร | krai |
| whose | ของใคร | kö:ng krai |

# Prepositions

Grammar

| | | |
|---|---|---|
| about | ประมาณ | bpra-maan |
| from | จาก | jàak |
| in, at | ใน, ที่ | nai, tîi |
| on | บน | bon |
| under | ข้างใต้ | kâang-dtâi |
| by/with: | โดย | duuoy |
| between | ระหว่าง | ra-wàang |
| without | ปราศจาก | bpràat-sa-jàak |
| except | ยกเว้น | yók-wén |
| inside | ข้างใน | kâang-nai |
| outside | ข้างนอก | kâang-nô:k |

# Public holidays

| | |
|---|---|
| 1 January | **New Year's Day** |
| 13–15 April | **Songkran Festival**  Thai New Year. Thai people all over the country celebrate at this time. On the streets people splash water at each other to cool themselves down during the hot season. The National Family Day also occurs at this time. |
| 1 May | **National Labour Day**  There is a celebration at Sanam Luang, Bangkok. |
| 12 August | **HM the Queen's Birthday**  The Queen's Birthday is also Mother's Day. |
| 5 December | **HM the King's Birthday**  Thai people gather at Sanam Luang in Bangkok on the evening of 5 December to celebrate this event. |

## A

|  |  |  |
|---|---|---|
| a(an) | หนึ่ง | nùng |
| about | ประมาณ | bpra-maan |
| above | ข้างบน | kâang-bon |
| to accept | รับ | ráp |
| do you accept Visa®? | คุณรับบัตรวีซ่าไหม | khun ráp bàt visa |
| accident | อุบัติเหตุ | ù-bàt-dti-hèet |
| ache | ปวด | bpùat |
| it aches | มันปวด | man bpùat |
| address | ที่อยู่ | tîi yùu |
| admission charge | ค่าธรรมเนียม | kâa-tam-niam |
| adult | ผู้ใหญ่ | pûu yài |
| aeroplane | เครื่องบิน | krûang bin |
| after | หลังจาก | paai-lăng |
| afternoon | บ่าย | bàai |
| this afternoon | บ่ายนี้ | bàai níi |
| in the afternoon | ช่วงบ่ายนี้ | chûang bàai níi |
| tomorrow afternoon | บ่ายพรุ่งนี้ | bàai prûng níi |
| again | อีกครั้ง | iik kráng |
| age | อายุ | aa-yú |
| agent | ตัวแทน | dtua-taen |
| estate agent | ตัวแทนขาย... | dtua-taen kăai |
|  | อสังหาริมทรัพย์ | a-săng-hăa-rim-ma-sáp |
| travel agent | บริษัททัวร์ | bò-ri-sàt |
| ago | เมื่อ...ที่แล้ว | tôːng-fiao |
| ahead | ข้างหน้า | pàan bpai láew |
| straight ahead | ตรงไปข้างหน้า | kâang nâa |
|  |  | dtrong bpai kâang nâa |
|  | หน้า | nâa |
| air conditioning | แอร์/เครื่องปรับอากาศ | air-condition |
| airport | สนามบิน | sà-năam-bin |
| alarm | ระบบเตือนภัย | na-bòb-dtuan-pai |
| alarm clock | นาฬิกาปลุก | naa-lí-gaa-bplùk |
| alcohol | เครื่องดื่มมึนเมา | krûang dùum |
|  | เมา | mun mao |

| English | Thai | |
|---|---|---|
| without alcohol | ไม่มีแอลกอฮอล์ | mâi mii láo |
| all | ทั้งหมด | táng-mòt |
| to be allergic to | ที่แพ้ | puum-páe |
| all right (OK) | ตกลง | dtòk-long (ok) |
| I'm all right | ฉันไม่เป็นไร | chan mâi bpen a-rai |
| alone | อยู่คนเดียว | yùu kon diao |
| always | ตลอดไป | dta-lòrd bpai |
| ambulance | รถพยาบาล | rót-pa-yaa-baan |
| America | อเมริกา | a-mee-ri-gaa |
| American | คนอเมริกา | kona-mee-ri-gaa |
| and | และ | láe |
| angry | โกรธ | gròot |
| I'm angry | ฉันโกรธ | chan gròot |
| another | อย่างอื่น | yàang ùun |
| another beer | เบียร์อีกขวด | beer ìik kùat |
| answer | คำตอบ | kam-tòrp |
| to answer | ตอบ | tòrp |
| answering machine | เครื่องตอบรับอัตโนมัติ | krûang tòrp ráp àt-tà-noo-mát |
| ants | มด | mót |
| any | บางอย่าง | bâang mái |
| apartment | อพาร์ตเมนท์ | a-páat-mént |
| apple | แอปเปิล | apple |
| apple juice | น้ำแอปเปิล | náam apple |
| April | เมษายน | mee-sǎa-yon |
| arm | แขน | kǎen |
| my arm hurts | ฉันเจ็บแขน | chan jèb kǎen |
| to arrest | โดนจับ | doon jàb |
| arrivals | ขาเข้า | kǎa-kâo |
| to arrive | มาถึง | maa tǔng |
| artist | ศิลปิน | sin-lá-bpin |
| ashtray | ที่เขี่ยบุหรี่ | tîi kìa bu-rìi |
| asthma | โรคหืด | rôok-hùut |
| at | ที่ | tîi |
| attack | จู่โจม/กำเริบ | jùu-joom/kam-rûrp |

English – Thai

# English – Thai

|  |  |  |
|---|---|---|
| *heart attack* | โรคหัวใจ | rôok hŭa-jai |
| attention | กำไร | kam-rúrp |
| attractive | ความสนใจ | kwaam-sŏn-jai |
| August | สวย/มีเสน่ห์ | sŭoy/mii sa-nèe |
| Australia | สิงหาคม | sĭng-hăa-kom |
| Australian | ประเทศออส เตรเลีย | bprà-têet-òt-sa-dtree-lia |
| Australian | คนออส เตรเลีย | kon òt-sa-dtree-lia |
| automatic car | รถเกียร์ออโต้ | rót-giia-auto |
| away | จากไป | jàak bpai |
| *please go away!* | กรุณาไปให้ พ้น | ka-ru-naa bpai hâi pón |
| **B** | | |
| baby | ทารก | taa-rók |
| baby food | อาหารทารก | aa-hăan taa-rók |
| babysitter | คนดูแลเด็ก | kon-duu-lae-dèk |
| back (of body) | หลัง | lăng |
| backpack | เป้ | bpê |
| bad | ไม่ดี | mâi dii |
| bag | กระเป๋า | grà-bpăo |
| baggage | กระเป๋าเดินทาง | grà-bpăo durn taang |
| baker's | คนทำขนมปัง | kon tam ka-nŏm bpang |
| ball | ลูกบอล | lûuk-bon |
| bandage | ผ้าพันแผล | pâa-pan-plăe |
| bank | ธนาคาร | ta-naa-kaan |
| bar | บาร์ | bar |
| barber | ช่างตัดผม | châang-dtàt-pŏm |
| bargain | ต่อรอง | dtòr rong |
| *no bargaining* | ไม่มีการต่อ รอง | mâi mii gaan dtòr rong |
| basket | ตะกร้า | dtà-grâa |
| bath | การอาบน้ำ | gaan-àap-náam |
| bathroom | ห้องอาบน้ำ | hôrng àap-náam |
| *where is the bathroom?* | ห้องน้ำอยู่ ที่ไหน | hôrng náam yùu tîi năi |
| *with bathroom* | มีห้องน้ำ | mii hôrng náam |

| English | Thai | |
|---|---|---|
| battery (for car) | แบตเตอรี่รถ | bàet-tur-rî-rót |
| (for torch, camera) | การไฟฉาย | tàan-fai-chǎai |
| bazaar | ตลาดนัด | dta-làat-nát |
| be | เป็น | bpen |
| beach | ชายหาด | chaai-hàat |
| beautiful | สวย | sǔay |
| bed | เตียง | dtiang |
| double bed | เตียงคู่ | dtiang-kûu |
| twin beds | เตียงเดี่ยวคู่ | dtiang-dìao kûu |
| bedclothes | ผ้าปูที่นอน | pâa-bpuu-tîi-nom |
| bedroom | ห้องนอน | hông-nom |
| double bedroom | ห้องเตียงคู่ | hông-dtiang-kûu |
| single bedroom | ห้องเตียงเดี่ยว | hông-dtiang-dìao |
| bee | ผึ้ง | pûng |
| beef | เนื้อวัว | núa-wua |
| beer | เบียร์ | beer |
| a glass of beer | เบียร์หนึ่งแก้ว | beer nùng gâew |
| a bottle of beer | เบียร์หนึ่งขวด | beer nùng kùat |
| before | ก่อนหน้า | gòn nâa |
| before 4 o'clock | ก่อนสี่โมง | gòn sìi moong |

| English | Thai | |
|---|---|---|
| before dinner | ก่อนอาหาร | gòn aa-hǎan |
| | ค่ำ | kâm |
| to begin | เริ่ม | rûm |
| behind | ข้างหลัง | kâang lǎng |
| to believe | เชื่อ | chûa |
| I don't believe | ฉันไม่เชื่อคุณ | chan mâi chûa |
| you | | khun |
| below | ข้างล่าง | kâang-lâang |
| belt | เข็มขัด | kěm-kàt |
| money belt | กระเป๋าเข็มขัด | grà-bpǎo kěm-kàt |
| | | kàt |
| seat belt | เข็มขัดนิรภัย | kěm-kàt ni-rá-pai |
| bend | กม | gom |
| beside | ข้าง | kâang |
| (next to) | ติดกับ | dtìd-kàp |
| best | ดีที่สุด | dii-tîi-sùt |
| better (than) | ดีกว่า | dii-gwàa |
| bicycle | จักรยาน | jàk-grà-yaan |
| big | ใหญ่ | yài |
| bigger | ใหญ่กว่า | yài gwàa |

# English – Thai

| | | |
|---|---|---|
| biggest | ใหญ่ที่สุด | yài tîi sùt |
| bill (invoice) | ใบเก็บเงิน | bai-gèb ngurn |
| bin (for rubbish) | ใบส่งของ | bai-sòng-kǒ:ng |
| bird | นก | nók |
| birthday | วันเกิด | wan-gùrt |
| happy birthday! | สุขสันต์วันเกิด | sùk-sǎn wan-gùrt |
| birthday card | การ์ดวันเกิด | gáat wan-gùrt |
| biscuits | บิสกิต | biscuit |
| a little bit | นิดหน่อย | níd-nòi |
| bite (insect, dog) | กัด | gàt |
| bitter (taste) | ขม | kǒm |
| black | ดำ | dam |
| blanket | ผ้าห่ม | pâa-hòm |
| to bleed | เลือดออก | lûat-òrk |
| blind (person) | ตาบอด | dtaa-bòrt |
| blinds (on window) | ที่กันแสง | tîi-gan-sǎeng |
| blister | บาดแผลพุพอง | plàe pú-porng |

| | | |
|---|---|---|
| blocked | ตัน | dtan |
| the sink is blocked | อ่างนี้มันตัน | àang níi dtan |
| blood | เลือด | lûat |
| blood group | เลือดกรุป | lûat-group |
| blood pressure | ความดันเลือด | kwaam dan lûat |
| blue | สีฟ้า | sǐi fáa |
| boarding card | บัตรผ่านขึ้นเครื่อง | bàt pàan bpra-tuu |
| boat | เรือ | ruua |
| boat trip | เดินทางทาง เรือ | durn-taang taang ruua |
| boiled (food) | ต้ม | dtôm |
| bone | กระดูก | grà-dùuk |
| book | หนังสือ | nǎng-sǔu |
| to book | จอง | jo:ng |
| I've booked | ฉันจองไว้ แล้ว | chan jo:ng wái láew |
| booking | การจอง | gaan jo:ng |
| bookshop | ร้านหนังสือ | ráan nǎng-sǔu |
| boots | รองเท้าบู๊ต | tíi show sín-káa |

| English | Thai | |
|---|---|---|
| boring | น่าเบื่อ | nâa-bùa |
| it's boring | มันน่าเบื่อ | man nâabùa |
| both | ทั้งคู่ | kûu |
| I'd like both | ฉันชอบทั้งคู่ | chan chôp táng kûu |
| bottle | ขวด | kùat |
| a bottle of water | น้ำหนึ่งขวด | náam nùng kùat |
| a bottle of wine | ไวน์หนึ่งขวด | wine nùng kùat |
| bottle opener | ที่เปิดขวด | tîi bpèrd kùat |
| box | กล่อง | glòng |
| box office | ห้องขายตั๋ว | hông kǎai dtǔa |
| boy | เด็กผู้ชาย | dèk pûu chaai |
| boyfriend | แฟน | faen |
| brandy | บรั่นดี | brandy |
| bread | ขนมปัง | ka-nŏm bpang |
| to break | หัก | hàk |
| to break down (car) | รถเสีย | rót sĭa |
| breakfast | อาหารเช้า | aa-hǎan cháao |

| English | Thai | |
|---|---|---|
| breakfast | | |
| included | รวมอาหารเช้า | ruam aa-hǎan cháao |
| to breathe | หายใจ | hǎai-jai |
| to bring | นำ | nam |
| British | อังกฤษ | ang-grìt |
| I'm British | ฉันเป็นคนอังกฤษ | chan bpen kon ang-grìt |
| brochure | แผ่นโฆษณา | pâen-koo-sà-naa |
| broken | เสีย | sĭa |
| broken down (car, machine) | เสีย | sĭa |
| brother (elder brother/younger brother) | พี่ชาย/ น้องชาย | pîi-chaai/ nóng-chaai |
| brown | สีน้ำตาล | sǐi-nám-dtaan |
| brush | แปรง | bpraeng |
| bucket | ถังน้ำ | tǎng náam |
| bulb (light) | หลอดไฟ | lòrdt-fai |
| burglary | ปล้น | bplôn |
| burn | ไหม้ | mâi |

# English – Thai

| to burn | เผา | pǎo |
|---|---|---|
| burnt | ไหม้ | mâi |
| it's burnt | มันไหม้ | man mâi |
| bus | รถบัส | rót-bus |
| business | ธุรกิจ | tú-rá-gìt |
| bus station | สถานีรถเมล์ | sa-tǎa-nii |
| bus stop | ป้ายรถเมล์ | bpâai rót-mee |
| busy | ยุ่ง | yûng |
| I'm busy | ฉันกำลังยุ่ง | chan gam-lang yûng |
| butcher's | คนขายเนื้อ | kon kǎai núa |
| butter | เนย | neei |
| to buy | ซื้อ | súu |
| by | โดย | duoy |
| by bus | โดยรถบัส | duoy rót-bus |
| by train | โดยรถไฟ | duoy rót-fai |

## C

| café | ร้านกาแฟ | ráan gaa-fae |
|---|---|---|
| cake | เค้ก | cake |
| cake shop | ร้านเค้ก | ráan-cake |
| to call (on phone) | โทรฯ | too-hǎa |
| camcorder | กล้องถ่ายวิดีโอ | glôːng tàai nǎng |
| camera | กล้องถ่ายรูป | glôːng tàai rûub |
| to camp | ออกค่าย | òrk-kâai |
| camp site | บริเวณค่าย | bo:-ri-ween kâai |
| no camping | ไม่มีการตั้งแคมป์ | mâi mii gaan tâng |
| | ตามบริเวณนี้ | kǎai bo:-ri-ween |
| | | nii |
| can (tin) | กระป๋อง | grà-bpǒːng |
| cancel | ยกเลิก | yók-lûrk |
| candle | เทียนไข | tian-kái |
| can opener | ที่เปิดกระป๋อง | tîi bpùrd grà- |
| | | bpǒ:ng |
| car | รถยนต์ | rót-yon |
| by car | โดยรถยนต์ | duoy rót-yon |
| car park | ที่จอดรถ | tîi jòrd rót |

| English | Thai | Pronunciation |
|---|---|---|
| car seat (for child) | ที่นั่งเด็ก | tîi nâng dék |
| car wash | ที่ล้างรถ | tîi láang rót |
| card | การ์ด | gáat |
| cards (playing) | ไพ่ | pâi |
| carpet (rug) | พรม | prom |
| carry | ถือ | tǔu |
| cash | เงินสด | ngurn-sòt |
| I have no cash | ฉันไม่มีเงินสด | chǎn mâi mii ngurn-sòt |
| to cash | เบิกเงิน | bùrg-ngurn |
| cash desk | โต๊ะเก็บเงิน | dtó gèp ngurn |
| castle | ปราสาท | bpra-sàat |
| cat | แมว | maew |
| caution | ระวัง | rá-wang |
| cave | ถ้ำ | tâm |
| CD | ซีดี | sii-dii |
| CD player | เครื่องเล่นซีดี | krûuang lên sii-dii |
| cemetery | ป่าช้า | pàa-cháa |
| central | ศูนย์กลาง | sǔun glaang |

| English | Thai | Pronunciation |
|---|---|---|
| central station | สถานีศูนย์กลาง | sà-tǎa-nii sǔun glaang |
| town centre | ใจกลางเมือง | jai glaang muang |
| certificate | ใบรับรอง | bai-ráp-rong |
| chain | สายโซ่ | sôo (to chain – lâam-sôo) |
| chair | เก้าอี้ | gâo-îi |
| champagne | แชมเปญ | chaem-bpeen |
| change (loose coins) | เศษสตางค์ | sèet-sa-taang |
| to change (money) | แลกเปลี่ยน | lâek-bplian |
| changing room | ห้องเปลี่ยนเสื้อผ้า | hôˑng bplian sûa-pâa |
| charge (fee) | ค่าธรรมเนียม | kâa-tam-niam |
| cheap | ถูก | tùuk |
| check | เช็ค | chék |
| to check in | เช็คอิน | chék-in |
| cheers! | ไชโย | chai-yo |
| cheese | เนยแข็ง | neei-kǎeng |

| chemist's | เภสัชกร | pee-sàt-cha-gorn |
| night duty | เภสัชกรราตรี | pee-sàt-cha-gorn |
| chemist | ร้านยา | ween-rórb-dùk |
| cheque | เช็ค | check |
| cheque book | สมุดเช็ค | sà-mùt check |
| traveller's | เช็คเดินทาง | check dum-taang |
| cheques | | |
| cherry | เชอร์รี่ | chur-rîi |
| chest (of body) | อก | òk |
| chewing gum | หมากฝรั่ง | màak-fà-ràng |
| chickenpox | อีสุกอีใส | ìi-sùk-ìi-sǎi |
| child | เด็ก | dèk |
| chips | มันฝรั่งทอด | man fà-ràng tôrt |
| chocolate | ช็อกโกแล็ต | chók-goo-làet |
| hot chocolate | ช็อกโกแล็ตร้อน | chók-goo-làet |
| | | rórn |
| chop (meat) | ชิ้น | sàp |
| Christmas | คริสต์มาส | krít-sa-mâat |
| church | โบสถ์ | bòot |
| cigar | ซิการ์ | si-gâa |

| cigarettes | บุหรี่ | bù-rìi |
| a packet of | บุหรี่หนึ่งซอง | bù-rìi nùng song |
| cigarettes | หนึ่ง | |
| cinema | โรงหนังอยู่ | nàng |
| where is the | ที่ไหน | roong-nǎng yùu |
| cinema? | | tîi nǎi? |
| city | เมือง | muang |
| city centre | ใจกลางเมือง | jai glaang muang |
| clean | ความสะอาด | kwaam sà-àat |
| it's not clean | มันไม่สะอาด | man mâi sà-àat |
| to clean | ทำความ | tam kwaam |
| | สะอาด | sà-àat |
| climbing | ปีน | bpin |
| to go climbing | ไปปีนเขา | bpai bpin kǎo |
| clock | นาฬิกา | naa-lí-gaa |
| close | ใกล้ | glâi |
| is it close by? | อยู่ใกล้ไหม | yùu glâi mái? |
| to close | ปิด | bpìd? |
| when does it | มันปิดเมื่อ, เมื่อไหร่ | man bpìd mûa- |
| close? | | rài? |

| English | Thai | Pronunciation |
|---|---|---|
| closed | ปิด | bpìd |
| clothes | เสื้อผ้า | sûa-pâa |
| coast | ฝั่งทะเล | fàng-tá-lee |
| coat | เสื้อคลุม | sûa-klum |
| cocoa | โกโก้ | goo-gôo |
| cockroach | แมลงสาบ | má-laeng-sàap |
| coconut | มะพร้าว | má-práao |
| coffee | กาแฟ | gaa-fae |
| *black coffee* | กาแฟดำ | gaa-fae-dam |
| *iced coffee* | กาแฟเย็น | chaa-dam-yen |
| *instant coffee* | กาแฟสำเร็จรูป | gaa-fae-sàm-rèt-rûub |
| coin | เหรียญ | rian |
| Coke® | โค้ก | Coke |
| cold | หวัด | wàt |
| *I have a cold* | ฉันเป็นหวัด | chan bpen wàt |
| *to be cold* | หนาว | nǎao |
| *I'm cold* | ฉันหนาว | chan nǎao |
| colour | สี | sǐi |
| comb | หวี | wǐi |
| to come (arrive) | มาถึง | maa tǔng |
| *come in!* | เข้ามา! | kâo-maa! |
| comfortable | สบาย | sà-baai |
| company (business) | บริษัท | bò-rí-sàt |
| compass | เข็มทิศ | kém-tít |
| complaint | ต่อว่า | dtòr-wâa |
| computer | คอมพิวเตอร์ | com-pu-ter |
| concert | คอนเสิร์ต | con-cert |
| conditioner (for hair) | ครีมนวดผม | cream-nûat-pŏm |
| condoms | ถุงยาง | tǔng-yaang |
| conference | การประชุม | gaan-bpra-chum |
| to confirm | ยืนยัน | yuun-yan |
| congratulations! | ยินดีด้วยครับ/ค่ะ | yin dii dûoy krab/kâ! |
| connection (train, plane) | ต่อ | dtòr |
| consulate | สถานกงสุล | sà-tǎan-gong-sǔn |

English – Thai

| English | Thai | |
|---|---|---|
| British consulate | สถานกงสุลอังกฤษ | sà-tǎan-gong-sùn ang-grìt |
| American consulate | สถานกงสุลอเมริกา | sà-tǎan-gong-sùn a-mee-rí-gaa |
| contact lens | คอนแท็คเลนส์ | kon-táek-len |
| contraceptive pill | ยาคุมกำเนิด | yaa-kum-gam-nèrt |
| to cook | ทำอาหาร | tam aa-hǎan |
| cooker | คนทำอาหาร | kon tam aa-hǎan |
| copy | การถ่ายเอกสาร | tàai èek-gà-sǎan |
| to copy (photocopy) | การถ่ายเอกสาร | tàai èek-gà-sǎan |
| corkscrew | ที่เปิดขวดไวน์ | tîi bpèrd wine |
| corner | หัวมุม | hǔa mum |
| cot | เปล | bplee |
| cost | ราคา | raa-kaa |
| how much does it cost? | ราคาเท่าไหร่? | raa-kaa tâo rài? |
| cotton (material) | ผ้าฝ้าย | pâa-fàai |
| to cough | ไอ | ai |

| English | Thai | |
|---|---|---|
| counter (desk) | เคาน์เตอร์ | count-ter |
| country (not town) | ชนบท | chon-na-bòt |
| couple (two people) | สามี-ภรรยา | sǎamii-panrayaa |
| crash (collision) | ชน | chon |
| crash helmet | หมวกกันน็อก | mùak gan nók |
| cream (dairy) | ครีม | cream |
| credit card | เครดิตการ์ด | kree-dìt-gàat |
| to cry (weep) | ร้องไห้ | róng-hâi |
| cucumber | แตงกวา | dtaeng-gwaa |
| cup | ถ้วย | tûai |
| cushion | เบาะ | bò: |
| customs | ศุลกากร | sǔn-lá-gaa-gorn |
| customs control | ด่านศุลกากร | dàan sǔn-lá-gaa-gorn |
| cut | ตัด | dtàt |
| to cut | ตัด | dtàt |
| to cycle (bicycle) | ขี่จักรยาน | kìi-jàk-grà-yaan |
| a cycle | วงจร | wong-jorn |

# D

| English | Thai | |
|---|---|---|
| daily | ประจำวัน | bprà-jam-wan |
| damage | เสียหาย | sia hăai |
| dance | การเต้นรำ | gaan dtên-ram |
| to dance | เต้นรำ | dtên-ram |
| danger | อันตราย | an-dta-raai |
| dangerous | อันตราย | an-dta-raai |
| dark | มืด | mûut |
| date (calendar) | วันที่ | wan-tîi |
| date of birth | วันเกิด | wan gèrt |
| daughter | ลูกสาว | lûuk săao |
| day | วัน | wan |
| every day | ทุกวัน | túk wan |
| deaf | หูหนวก | hŭu-nùuak |
| decaffeinated coffee | กาแฟไม่มี คาเฟอีน | gaa-fae mâi mii kaa-fee-in |
| December | ธันวาคม | tan-waa-kom |
| deck chair | เก้าอี้ผ้าใบ | gâo-îi-pâa-bai |
| deep | ลึก | lúk |
| delay | ล่าช้า | lâa-cháa |

| English | Thai | |
|---|---|---|
| delicious | อร่อย | aròy |
| *this is delicious!* | อันนี้อร่อยมาก | an níi aròy mâak |
| dentist | หมอฟัน | mŏr fan |
| dentures | ฟันปลอม | fan-bplorm |
| deodorant | ยาดับกลิ่นตัว | yaa-dàp-glìn-dtua |
| department store | ห้างสรรพสินค้า | Hâang-sàp-pa-sĭn-káa |
| departures | ขาออก | kăa òrk |
| deposit | ฝาก | fàak |
| dessert | ของหวาน | kŏng-wăan |
| detergent | ผงซักฟอก | pŏng-sák-fôrk |
| diabetic | โรคเบาหวาน | rôok-bao-wăan |
| dialling code | รหัสโทรศัพท์ | rá-hàt too-rá-sàp |
| diamond | เพชร | pét |
| diarrhoea | โรคท้องเสีย | rôok tóng-sĭa |
| diary | ไดอารี่ | dai-aa-rîi |
| dictionary | พจนานุกรม | pót-jà-naa-nú-grom |
| diesel | ดีเซล | dii-sell |

English – Thai

| diet | การควบคุม | gaan kûap-kum |
| | อาหาร | aa-hăan |
| I'm on a diet | ฉันกำลังลด | chan gamlang lót |
| | อาหารหนัก | náam nàk |
| different | แตกต่าง | dtaek-dtàang |
| difficult | ยาก | yâak |
| it's difficult | มันยาก | man yâak |
| dinghy | เรือเล็ก | ruua lék |
| dining room | ห้องทานอาหาร | hông taan |
| | | aa-hăan kâm |
| dinner (evening meal) | อาหารค่ำ | |
| direct | ตรง | dtrong |
| direct flight | บินตรง | bin dtrong |
| directory (telephone) | สมุด | sà-mùt too-rá- |
| | โทรศัพท์ | sàp |
| dirty | สกปรก | sòk-gà-bpròk |
| disabled (person) | คนพิการ | kon pí-gaan |
| disco | เธค | têk |
| discount | ส่วนลด | sùan lót |

| disease | โรค | rôok |
| disinfectant | มาจากเชื้อโรค | yaa-kâa-chúa- |
| | | rôok |
| distilled water | น้ำกลั่น | náam-glàn |
| to dive | ดำน้ำ | dam náam |
| divorced | หย่า | yàa |
| I'm divorced | ฉันเป็นหม้าย | chan bpen mâai |
| dizzy | เวียนหัว | wiian hŭa |
| I feel dizzy | ฉันรู้สึก | chan rúu-sùk |
| | เวียนหัว | wiian hŭa |
| doctor | หมอ | mŏr |
| documents | เอกสาร | èek-gà-săan |
| dog | หมา | măa |
| doll | ตุ๊กตา | dtúk-gà-dtaa |
| door | ประตู | bpra-tuu |
| double bed | เตียงคู่ | dtiang kûu |
| double room | ห้องคู่ | hông kûu |
| downstairs | ชั้นล่าง | Chán lâang |
| dozen | หนึ่งโหล | nùng-lŏo |
| drain | ระบายน้ำ | rá-baai-náam |

| | | |
|---|---|---|
| drawer | ลิ้นชัก | lín-chák |
| dress | กระโปรงชุด | gra-bproong-chút |
| drink | ดื่ม | dùum |
| to drink | การดื่ม | gaan dùum |
| drinking water | น้ำดื่ม | náam dùum |
| to drive | ขับ | kàp |
| driver | คนขับ | kon kàp |
| driving licence | ใบขับขี่ | bai-kàp-kìi |
| to drown | จมน้ำ | jom náam |
| drug | ยา | yaa |
| drunk | เมา | mao |
| I'm drunk | ฉันเมา | chan mao |
| dry | ทำให้แห้ง | tam-hâi-hâeng |
| dry-cleaner's | ร้านซักแห้ง | ráan sák hâeng |
| dust | ฝุ่น | fùn |
| duty-free | ร้านสินค้าปลอดภาษี | bplòrt paa-sǐi |

## E

| | | |
|---|---|---|
| ear | หู | hǔu |
| earache | หูเจ็บ | hǔujèb |
| I have earache | หูเจ็บเป็น | hǔu chan jèb |
| early | เช้าตรู่ | cháao cháao |
| earrings | ต่างหู | dtàang-hǔu |
| earthquake | แผ่นดินไหว | pàen-din-wâi |
| east | ตะวันออก | dtà-wan-òrk |
| easy | ง่าย | ngâai |
| to eat | กิน | gin |
| egg | ไข่ | kài |
| elastic band | ยางยืด | yaang-yûud |
| electric | ไฟฟ้า | fai-fáa |
| electric razor | มีดโกนหนวดไฟฟ้า | mîit-goon fai-fáa |
| e-mail | อีเมล | e-mail |
| embassy | สถานทูต | sa-tǎan-tûut |
| American embassy | สถานทูต | sa-tǎan-tûut |
| | อเมริกา | a-mee-rí-gaa |
| British embassy | สถานทูตอังกฤษ | sa-tǎan-tûut |
| | อังกฤษ | ang-grìt |

# English – Thai

|  |  |  |
|---|---|---|
| emergency | ฉุกเฉิน | chùk-chĕrn |
| empty | ว่างเปล่า | wâang bplàao |
| end | จบ | jòb |
| engaged (to be married) | หมั้น | mân |
| it's engaged (phone, toilet) | มันไม่ว่าง | man mâi wâang |
| engine | เครื่องยนต์ | krêuang-yon |
| England | อังกฤษ | ang-grìt |
| English | คนอังกฤษ | kon ang-grìt |
| I'm English | ฉันเป็นคนอังกฤษ | chan bpen kon ang-grìt |
| enough | เพียงพอ | piang-por |
| it's not enough | มันไม่พอ | man mâi por |
| enquiry desk | ติดต่อสอบถาม | dtid-dtòr sòrb-tăam |
| to enter | การเข้างาน | gaan kâo bpai |
| entertainment | การบันเทิง | gaan ban-turng |
| entrance | ทางเข้า | taang kâo |
| entrance fee | ค่าเข้า | kâa kâo |

|  |  |  |
|---|---|---|
| envelope | ซองจดหมาย | song-jòt-măai |
| escape | หลบหนี | lòp nĭi |
| fire escape | ทางหนีไฟ | taang-nĭi-fai |
| Europe | ยุโรป | yú-ròop |
| evening | ตอนเย็น | dtorn yen |
| this evening | เย็นนี้ | yen níi |
| tomorrow evening | เย็นพรุ่งนี้ | yen prûng níi |
| evening meal | อาหารเย็น | aa-hăan yen |
| every | ทุกๆ | túk túk |
| every day | ทุกทุกวัน | túk túk wan |
| every year | ทุกทุกปี | túk túk bpii |
| everyone | ทุกๆคน | túk túk kon |
| excellent | ยอดเยี่ยม | yôt-yîam |
| exchange | และเปลี่ยน | lâek bplian |
| exchange rate | อัตราแลกเปลี่ยน | àt-dtraa lâek bplian |
| exciting | น่าตื่นเต้น | nâa-dtùun-dtên |
| excuse me! | ขอโทษครับ/ค่ะ | kŏr-tôot krab/kà! |

| English | Thai | |
|---|---|---|
| exhibition | นิทรรศการ | ní-tàt-sà-gaan |
| exit | ทางออก | taang òrk |
| where is the exit? | ทางออกอยู่ ไหน | taang òrk yùu nǎi? |
| emergency exit | ทางออกฉุก เฉิน | taang òrk chùk-chœœn |
| expensive | แพง | paeng |
| to expire | หมดอายุ | mòt aa-yú |
| to explain | อธิบาย | à-tí-baai |
| please explain | กรุณาอธิบาย | ga-rú-naa à-tí-baai |
| extra | เพิ่ม | pœ̂œm |
| eye | ตา | dtaa |
| **F** | | |
| face | หน้า | nâa |
| factory | โรงงาน | roong-ngaan |
| to faint | เป็นลม | bpen lom |
| to fall | ตก | dtòk |
| family | ครอบครัว | krôrp-krua |
| famous | มีชื่อเสียง | mii chûu-siang |
| fan | แฟน | faen |
| far | ไกล | glai |
| is it far? | ไกลไหม | glai mái? |
| fare (train, bus, etc.) | ค่าโดยสาร | kâa duoy-sǎan |
| farm | ฟาร์ม | farm |
| farmer | ชาวนา | chao-naa |
| fashion | แฟชั่น | fae-chân |
| fast | เร็ว | reo |
| fat (person) | อ้วน | ûan |
| father | พ่อ | pôr |
| my father | พ่อของฉัน | pôr kǒrng chan |
| father-in-law | พ่อตา | pôr dtaa |
| fault (defect) | มีตำหนิ | mii dtam-ni |
| favourite | โปรดปราน | bproot-bpraan |
| February | กุมภาพันธ์ | gum-paa-pan |
| feel | รู้สึก | rúu-sùk |
| I feel sick | ฉันรู้สึกคลื่น ไส้ | chan rúu-sùk klûun-sâi |

# English - Thai

|  |  |  |  |  |  |
|---|---|---|---|---|---|
| I feel tired | ฉันเหนื่อย | chan nùai | the first train | รถไฟเที่ยวแรก | rót fai tîao râek |
| ferry | เรือข้ามฟาก | rua-kâam-fâak | the first bus | รถบัสเที่ยวแรก | rót bus tîao râek |
| few | นิดหน่อย | níd-nòi | first aid | ปฐมพยาบาล | bpà-tǒm pa-yaa-baan |
| fiancé(e) | คู่หมั้น | kûu-mân | first class | ชั้นหนึ่ง | chán nùng |
| to fill (up) | เติม | dterm | first floor | ชั้นหนึ่ง | chán nùng |
| fill it up! | เติมให้เต็ม! | dterm hâi dtem! | fish | ปลา | bplaa |
| film | ฟิล์ม | film | to fish | ตกปลา | dtòk bplaa |
| filter | ที่กรอง | tîi grorng | fisherman | คนจับปลา | kon jàp bplaa |
| to find | ค้นหา | kón-hǎa | fit | พอดี | por-dii |
| fine (to be paid) | ค่าปรับ | kâa pràp | fix | ซ่อม | sôm |
| fine (weather) | อากาศดี | aa-gàat dii | flash (for camera) | แฟลช | flash |
| finish | เสร็จ | sèt | flat (apartment) | เฟล็ต | flat |
| fire | ไฟ | fai | flat | แบน | baen |
| fire alarm | สัญญาณเตือนไฟ | sǎn-yaan dtuan fai | flavour | รส | rót |
| fire brigade | สถานีดับเพลิง | sà-tǎa-nii-dàp-plurng | flight | เที่ยวบิน | tîao-bin |
| fire exit | ทางหนีไฟ | taang nǐi fai | flood | น้ำท่วม | náam-tûam |
| fireworks | พลุไฟ | plú-fai | floor | ชั้น | chán |
| first | ครั้งแรก | kráng râek | | | |

| | | |
|---|---|---|
| flour | แป้ง | bpâeng |
| flower | ดอกไม้ | dòk-máai |
| flu | ไข้หวัดใหญ่ | kâi-wàt-yài |
| fly | บิน | bin |
| to fly | การบิน | gaan bin |
| fog | หมอก | mòrk |
| folder | แฟ้ม | fáem |
| to follow | ตาม | dtaam |
| food | อาหาร | aa-hǎan |
| foot | เท้า | táo |
| football (game) | ฟุตบอล | fút-bon |
| for | สำหรับ | sǎm-ràp |
| for me | สำหรับฉัน | sǎm-ràp chan |
| for sale | ขาย | kǎai |
| forbidden | ต้องห้าม | dtông-hâam |
| forecast (weather) | พยากรณ์อากาศ | pa-yaa-gorn aa-gàat |
| foreign | คนต่างชาติ | kon dtaang-châat |
| forest | ป่า | bpàa |
| forever | ตลอดไป | dta-lòrd-bpai |

| | | |
|---|---|---|
| to forget | ลืม | luum |
| fork (for eating) | ส้อม | sôm |
| forward(s) | ส่งต่อ | sòng dtòr |
| free (unoccupied) | ว่าง | wâang |
| free (costing nothing) | ฟรี | frii |
| freezer | ช่องแช่แข็ง | chôhng-châe-yen |
| French | คนฝรั่งเศส | kon fa-ràng-sèet |
| frequent | ถี่, บ่อย | tìi, bòi |
| fresh | สด | sòt |
| is it fresh? | มันสดไหม | man sòt mǎi? |
| fresh fruit | ผลไม้สด | pònla-máai sòt |
| fresh vegetables | ผักสด | pàk sòt |
| fresh milk | นมสด | nom sòt |
| fresh fish | ปลาสด | bplaa-sòt |
| Friday | วันศุกร์ | wan-sùk |
| fridge | ตู้เย็น | tûu-yen |
| fried (food) | ทอด | tôrt |
| friend | เพื่อน | pûan |
| from | จาก | jàak |
| | | see GRAMMAR |

# English – Thai

| | | | | |
|---|---|---|---|---|
| front | ข้างหน้า | kâang-nâa | | |
| front door | ประตูหน้า | bpra-dtuu nâa | | |
| frozen | แช่แข็ง | châe-kǎeng | | |
| fruit | ผลไม้ | pǒn-lá-máai | | |
| fruit juice | น้ำผลไม้ | náam pǒn-lá-máai | | |
| fruit salad | สลัดผลไม้ | sà-làd pǒn-lá-máai | | |
| fuel | เชื้อเพลิง | chúa pləəng | | |
| full | เต็ม | dtem | | |
| furniture | เฟอร์นิเจอร์ | fur-ní-ture | | |

## G

| | | | | |
|---|---|---|---|---|
| gallery (art) | หองแสดง | hɔ̌ɔng sa-daeng | | |
| game (sport) | คีกะ | gii-laa | | |
| garden | สวน | sǔan | | |
| garlic | กระเทียม | grà-tiam | | |
| gas | แก๊ส | gáet | | |
| gate | ทางเข้า | taang-kâo | | |
| genuine | แท้ | táe | | |
| German | คนเยอรมัน | kon yur-rà-man | | |

| | | | | |
|---|---|---|---|---|
| Germany | เยอรมันนี | yur-rà-man | | dâai |
| to get | เอา | gaan kâo bpai súu | | |
| to get into | การเข้าไปสู่ | | | |
| to get on board | ขึ้นเรือ | kûn ruua | | |
| to get off (bus, etc.) | ลงรถ | long rót | | |
| gift | ของขวัญ | kɔ̌ɔng-kwǎn | | |
| girl | เด็กผู้หญิง | dèk pûu-yǐng | | |
| girlfriend | แฟน | faen | | |
| to give | ให้ | hâi | | |
| (give back) | ให้กลับ | hâi glàb | | |
| give way | ให้ทาง | hâi taang | | |
| glass (for drink) | แก้ว | gâew | | |
| a glass of water | น้ำหนึ่งแก้ว | náam nùng gâew | | |
| a glass of wine | ไวน์หนึ่งแก้ว | wine nùng gâew | | |
| to go | ไป | bpai | | |
| to go back | กลับไป | glàb bpai | | |
| to go in | เข้าไป | kâo bpai | | |
| to go out | ออกไป | ɔ̀ɔk bpai | | |
| gold | ทอง | tɔɔng | | |

| English | Thai | Pronunciation |
|---|---|---|
| golf | กอล์ฟ | golf |
| golf ball | ลูกกอล์ฟ | lûuk golf |
| golf club | กอล์ฟคลับ | golf club |
| good | ดี | dii |
| goodbye | ไปก่อนนะ | bpai kòn ná |
| good day | สวัสดี | sà-wàd-dii |
| goodnight | ราตรีสวัสดิ์ | raa-trii-sà-wàd |
| grandfather (paternal, maternal) | ปู่, ตา | bpùu, dtaa |
| grandmother (paternal, maternal) | ย่า, ยาย | yâa, yaai |
| grapes | องุ่น | a-ngùn |
| greasy | มัน | man |
| green | เขียว | kĭao |
| greengrocer's | ร้านขายผัก | ráan kăai pàk |
| grey | สีเทา | sĭi tao |
| grilled | ย่าง | yâang |

| English | Thai | Pronunciation |
|---|---|---|
| grocer's | ร้านขายของชำ | ráan kăai kŏng cham |
| group (of people) | กลุ่ม | glùm |
| guarantee | รับรอง | ráp-rong |
| guest | แขก | kàek |
| guest-house | บ้านเช่า | bâan châo |
| guide/ | คู่มือแนะแนว | kûu-muu |
| guidebook | | nâe-nam |
| guided tour | ทัวร์นำเที่ยว | tuua-nam-tîao |

## H

|  |  |  |
|---|---|---|
| hair | ผม | pŏm |
| hair dryer | ที่เป่าผม | tîi pào pŏm |
| hairbrush | แปรงหวีผม | bpraeng wĭi pŏm |
| haircut | ตัดผม | dtàt-pŏm |
| hairdresser | ช่างทำผม | châang tam pŏm |
| half | ครึ่ง | krûng |
| half bottle | ครึ่งขวด | krûng kùat |
| half an hour | ครึ่งชั่วโมง | krûng chûa moong |
| ham | แฮม | haem |

# English – Thai

|  |  |  |
|---|---|---|
| hand | มือ | muu |
| hand luggage | กระเป๋าถือ | grà-bpǎo-tǔu |
| handbag | กระเป๋าถือถือ | grà-bpǎo-muu-tǔu |
| hand-made | ทำด้วยมือ | tam-dûoy-muu |
| to hear | เกิดขึ้น | gèrt-kûn |
| what happened? | เกิดอะไรขึ้น? | gèrt-à-rai-kûn? |
| happy | ความสุข | kwaam-sùk |
| hard (tough) | ยาก | yâak |
| hat | หมวก | mùak |
| he | เขา | kǎo |
| head | หัว | hǔa |
| headache | ปวดหัว | bpùat-hǔa |
| I've got a headache | ฉันปวดหัว | chan-bpùat-hǔa |
| to hear | ได้ยิน | dâai-yin |
| heart | หัวใจ | hǔa-jai |
| heating | ทำความร้อน | tam-kwaam-rórn |
| heavy | หนัก | nàk |
| height | ความสูง | kwaam-sǔung |
| hello | สวัสดี | Sà-Wad-Dii |

|  |  |  |
|---|---|---|
| help! | ช่วยด้วย | chûai-dûoy! |
| to help | ช่วย | chûai |
| herbs | สะมุนไพร | sà-mǔn-prai |
| here | ที่นี่ | tîi-nîi |
| high | สูง | sǔung |
| high blood pressure | ความดันสูง | kwaam-dan |
| high chair | โต๊ะอาหารรับเด็ก | dtó sǎm-ràp dèk |
| to hire | เช่า | châo |
| to hitch-hike | โบกรถ | bòok-rót |
| holiday | วันหยุด | wan yùd |
| home | บ้าน | bâan |
| honey | น้ำผึ้ง | náam-pûng |
| honeymoon | น้ำผึ้งพระจันทร์ | náam pûng prá-jan |
| horse | ม้า | máa |
| hospital | โรงพยาบาล | roong-pa-yaa-baan |
| hot | ร้อน | rórn |

| English | Thai | |
|---|---|---|
| it's too hot | มันร้อนเกินไป | man rón gum bpai |
| hotel | โรงแรม | roong-raem |
| hour | ชั่วโมง | chûa-moong |
| house | บ้าน | bâan |
| how? | อย่างไร? | yàang-rai? |
| how much? | เท่าไหร่ | tâo-rài? |
| how many? | จำนวนเท่าไหร่ | jam-nuan tâo-rài? |
| how are you? | คุณสบายดีหรือ? | khun sà baai dii rǔu? |
| hungry | หิว | hiu |
| I'm hungry | หิวแล้ว | chan hiu |
| hurry | เร็ว เร็ว | reo reo |
| I'm in a hurry | ฉันกำลังรีบ | chan gamlang rîib |
| hurt | เจ็บ | jèb |
| it hurts | มันเจ็บ | man jèb |
| husband | สามี | săamii |
| my husband | สามีของฉัน | săamii kǒng chan |

| English | Thai | |
|---|---|---|
| I | ฉัน | chan |
| ice | น้ำแข็ง | náam kǎeng |
| ice cream | ไอศกรีม | ai-sa-kriim |
| iced coffee | กาแฟเย็น | gaa-fae-yen |
| iced tea | ชาเย็น | chaa-yen |
| iced water | น้ำแข็งเปล่า | náam kǎeng bplàao |
| identification card | บัตรประจำตัว | bàt pra jam dtua |
| ill | ป่วย | bpùai |
| I'm ill | ฉันป่วย | chan bpùai |
| immediately | โดยทันที | duay tan-tii |
| important | สำคัญ | săm-kan |
| impossible | เป็นไปไม่ได้ | bpen bpai mâi dâai |
| it's impossible | มันเป็นไปไม่ได้ | man bpen bpai mâi dâai |
| included | รวม | ruam |
| indigestion | อาหารไม่ย่อย | aa-hăan-mâi-yôi |
| infection | อักเสบ | àk-seep |

# English - Thai

| English | Thai | Pronunciation |
|---|---|---|
| information | ข้อมูล | kôr-moon |
| information | ติดต่อสอบถาม | dtid-dtòr |
| office | ถาม | sòrb-tăam |
| injured | บาดเจ็บ | bàat-jèb |
| I've been injured | ฉันบาดเจ็บ | chan bàat-jèb |
| insect | แมลง | ma-laeng |
| insect bite | แมลงกัด | ma-laeng-gàt |
| insect repellent | ยากันแมลง | yaa-gan-ma-laeng |
| instant coffee | กาแฟสำเร็จรูป | gaa-fae săm-rèt-rûub |
| insurance | ประกัน | bpra-gan |
| interesting | น่าสนใจ | nâa-sŏn-jai |
| international | สากล | săa-gon |
| interpreter | ล่าม | lâam |
| to invite | เชิญ | chun |
| invoice | ใบส่งของ | bai-sòng-kŏng |
| Ireland | ประเทศไอร์แลนด์ | bprà-têet-ai-laen |
| Irish | คนไอริช | kon-ai-írsh |

| English | Thai | Pronunciation |
|---|---|---|
| iron (metal) | ธาตุเหล็ก | tâat lèk |
| iron (for clothes) | เตารีด | dtao-rîit |
| island | เกาะ | gò: |
| it | มัน | man |
| itch | คัน | kan |

## J

| English | Thai | Pronunciation |
|---|---|---|
| jacket | เสื้อแจ็กเก็ต | sûa jáek-gét |
| leather jacket | เสื้อหนัง | sûa năng |
| jam (food) | แยม | yaem |
| January | มกราคม | má-ga-raa-kom |
| jar | กระปุก | grà-bpùk |
| jeans | ยีนส์ | yiin |
| jellyfish | แมงกะพรุน | maeng-gà-prun |
| jewellery | เครื่องประดับ | krûang-bprà-dàb |
| Jewish | ยิว | yui |
| I'm Jewish | ฉันเป็นคนยิว | chan bpen kon yui |
| job | งาน | ngaan |
| joke | ล้อเล่น | lór-lên |

| English | Thai | |
|---|---|---|
| journalist | เจ้าหน้าหนังสือพิมพ์ | nák-nǎng-sǔu-pim |
| journey | การเดินทาง | gaan dum-taang |
| juice | น้ำผลไม้ | náam pǒnla-mái |
| orange juice | น้ำส้ม | náam sôm |
| tomato juice | น้ำมะเขือเทศ | náam má-kǔa-têet |
| July | กรกฎาคม | gà-rá-gà-daa-kom |
| June | มิถุนายน | mí-tù-naa-yon |
| **K** | | |
| to keep | เก็บ | gèb |
| key | กุญแจ | gun-jae |
| kind | ใจดี | jai dii |
| you're very kind | คุณใจดีมาก | khun jai dii mâak |
| to kiss | จูบ | jùup |
| kitchen | ห้องครัว | hông krua |
| knee | เข่า | kào |
| knife | มีด | mîit |
| to know | รู้ | rúu |

| English | Thai | |
|---|---|---|
| *I know* | *ฉันรู้* | chan rúu |
| *I don't know* | *ฉันไม่รู้* | chan mâi rúu |
| **L** | | |
| ladies' (toilet) | ห้องน้ำ | hông-náam |
| | สุภาพสตรี | sù-pâap-sà-dtrii |
| larger | ใหญ่กว่า | yài gwàa |
| lake | ทะเลสาบ | tá-lee sàap |
| lamp | โคมไฟ | koom-fai |
| land | จอด | jòrt |
| landing | ลงจอด | long jòrt |
| late | สาย | sǎai |
| *sorry I'm late* | ขอโทษที่มาสาย | Kǒr-tôot tîi sǎai |
| later | วันหลัง | wan lǎng |
| laundry service | บริการซักรีด | bo-ri-gaan sák-rît |
| lawyer | ทนาย | tá-naai |
| leather | หนัง | nǎng |
| to leave | จาก | jàak |
| left | ทิ้ง | tíng |

# English – Thai

| English | Thai | | | | |
|---|---|---|---|---|---|
| left-luggage office | ที่ติดตอลัม | tîi dtìd-dtòr | lipstick | ลินสตีก | lip-sa-tick |
| leg | การะงาน | sâm-paa-rá hǎai | to listen to | ฟัง | fang |
| lemonade | ขา | kǎa | litter (rubbish) | ยยะ | kà-yà |
| to lend | น้ำมะนาว | náam ma-naow | little (small) | เล็ก | lék |
| to let (allow) | ให้ยืม | hâi yuum | just a little, please | ขอนิดเดียว ครับ/คะ | kŏr níd-diao kráb/kà |
| licence (driving) | ให้ | hâi | to live | อาศัย | aa-sǎi |
| lifeboat | ใบอนุญาต | bai-a-nú-yâat | I live in London | ฉันอาศัยที่ ลอนดอน | chan aa-sǎi tîi London |
| life jacket | เรือกูภย | ruua gûu-pai | | | |
| lifeguard | เสื้อชูชีพ | sûa-chuu-chîip | lock | ล็อค | lock |
| lift (elevator) | หนวยกูภย | nùai gûu-pai | to lock | ล็อค | lock |
| light (illumination) | ลิฟท | líf | locker (for luggage) | ท่าการล็อค | tam gaan lock |
| light bulb | ไฟส่องสว่าง | fai sòng-sa-wàng | | ล็อคเกอร | lock-ger |
| lighter (cigarette) | ลอดไฟ | lòrd-fai | long | หาน | naan |
| to like | ไฟฉแชค | fai-shâek | to look after someone | ดูแล | duu-lae |
| I like coffee | ชอบ | chôrp | | | |
| | ฉันชอบกาแฟ | chan chôrp | to look for | มองหา | mo:ng-hǎa |
| I don't like coffee | ฉันไม่ชอบ | chan mâi chô:p | lost | หาย | hǎai |
| | กาแฟ | gaa-fae | lot | มาก | mâak |
| linen | ผาลินิน | pâa linin | a lot | มากมาก | mâak mâak |

English – Thai

| | | |
|---|---|---|
| lotion | โลชั่น | lo-tion |
| loud | ดัง | dang |
| to love | รัก | rák |
| I love you | ฉันรักคุณ | chan rák khun |
| lovely | น่ารัก | nâa-rák |
| lucky | โชคดี | chôok-dii |
| luggage | กระเป๋า | grà-bpǎo durn |
| lunch | เดินทาง | taang |
| | อาหารกลางวัน | aa-hǎan glaang wan |
| **M** | | |
| maid | คนรับใช้ | kon ráp chái |
| main course | อาหารหลัก | aa-hǎan-làk |
| (of meal) | | |
| to make | ทำ | tam |
| man | ผู้ชาย | pôu chaai |
| manager | ผู้จัดการ | pôu-jàt-gaan |
| map | แผนที่ | pǎen-tîi |
| March | มีนาคม | mii-naa-kom |

| | | |
|---|---|---|
| married | แต่งงาน | dtàeng-ngaan |
| match (game) | เกมส์ | game |
| matches (light) | ไม้ขีด | máai-kìit |
| maximum | ความเร็วสูง | kwaam reo sǔung |
| speed | สุด | sùt |
| May | พฤษภาคม | prút-sa-paa-kom |
| meal | อาหาร | aa-hǎan |
| mean | หมายถึง | mǎai tǔng |
| measure | วัด | wát |
| meat | เนื้อ | núa |
| medicine | ยา | yaa |
| to meet | พบ | póp |
| meeting | การประชุม | gaan bpra-chum |
| menu | รายการ | raai-gaan |
| message | ข้อความ | kôr-kwaam |
| meter (taxi) | มิเตอร์ | mi-dtur |
| microwave | ไมโครเวฟ | mai-cro-wave |
| (oven) | | |
| midday | เที่ยงวัน | tîang wan |
| middle | กลาง | glaang |

# English – Thai

|  |  | |  |  | |
|---|---|---|---|---|---|
| midnight | เที่ยงคืน | tîang kuun | tomorrow | พรุ่งนี้ตอนเช้า | prûng níi cháao |
| milk | นม | nom | morning | ตอนเช้า | cháao |
| mineral water | น้ำแร่ | náam râe | mosque | สุเหร่า | sù-rào |
| mints | ลูกอมรสมินต์ | bai-sa-rà-nàe | mosquito net | มุ้ง | múng |
| minute | นาที | naa-tii | mosquitoes | ยุง | yung |
| mirror | กระจก | grà-jòk | mother | แม่ | mâe |
| miss (plane, train) | พลาด | plâad | mother-in-law | แม่ยาย | mâe-yaai |
| missing (thing) | หาย | hǎai | motorway | ทางด่วน | taang dùan |
| mistake | ผิด | pìd | mountain | ภูเขา | puu-kǎo |
| Monday | วันจันทร์ | wan-jan | mouse | หนู | nǔu |
| money | เงิน | ngum | moustache | หนวด | nùat |
| month | เดือน | duan | mouth | ปาก | bpàak |
| moon | พระจันทร์ | prá-jan | much | มาก | mâak |
| more | มากขึ้น | mâak kûn | how much? | เท่าไหร่ | tâo-rài? |
| some more... | ขอเพิ่มอีก | kǒr pǔm ìik nòi | too much | มากเกินไป | mâak bpai |
| | หน่อย | | it's too much | | |
| morning | ตอนเช้า | dtorn cháao | (too expensive) | มันแพงเกินไป | man paeng gun bpai |
| in the morning | ในตอนเช้า | nai dtorn cháao | museum | พิพิธภัณฑ์ | pí-pít-ta-pan |
| this morning | เช้านี้ | cháao níi | music shop | ร้านเพลง | ráan pleeng |
| | | | Muslim | อิสลาม | ìt-sa-laam |

|  |  |  |
|---|---|---|
| mustard | มัสตาร์ด | mát-sa-tàad |
| **N** | | |
| nail (metal) | ตะปู | dtà-bpuu |
| nail polish | น้ำยาทาเล็บ | náam-yaa-taa-lép |
| nail polish remover | น้ำยาลงเล็บ | náam-yaa-láang |
| name | ชื่อ | chûu |
| my name is | ฉันชื่อ | chan chûu |
| napkin | ผ้าเช็ดปาก | pâa chét bpàak |
| narrow | แคบ | kâep |
| nationality | สัญชาติ | sàn-châat |
| navy blue | สีกรมท่า | sii krom-mà-tâa |
| near | ใกล้ | glâi |
| is it near? | มันใกล้ไหม? | man glâi mái? |
| necessary | จำเป็น | jam-bpen |
| neck | คอ | kor |
| to need | ต้องการ | dtông gaan |
| I need... | ฉันต้องการ | chan dtông gaan... |
| I need a car | ฉันต้องการรถ | chan dtông gaan rót |
| I need to go | ฉันต้องการไป | chan dtông bpai |
| needle | เข็ม | kěm |
| neighbour | เพื่อนบ้าน | pûan bâan |
| nephew | หลานชาย | lǎan-chaai |
| never | ไม่เคย | mâi keei |
| new | ใหม่ | mài |
| news | ข่าว | kàao |
| newspaper | หนังสือพิมพ์ | nǎng-sǔu-pim |
| New Year | ปีใหม่ | bpii mài |
| New Zealand | นิวซีแลนด์ | niu-sii-laen |
| next | ต่อไป | dtòr bpai |
| next to | ติดกับ | dtìd-gàb |
| nice | ดี | dii |
| it's very nice | มันดีมาก | man dii mâak |
| niece | หลานสาว | lǎan sǎao |
| night | กลางคืน | glaang-kuun |
| last night | เมื่อคืน | mûa kuun |
| nightclub | ไนท์คลับ | night-club |

| English | Thai | Pronunciation |
|---|---|---|
| no | ไม่ | mâi |
| no, thanks | ไม่ครับ / คะ ขอบคุณ | mâi krab/kà kôrb-kun |
| noisy | หนวกหู | nûak hŭu |
| non-alcoholic | ไม่มีของ | mâi mii kŏng |
| a non-alcoholic drink | มึนเมา เครื่องดื่มไม่มีแอลกอฮอล์ | mun-mao krêuang dùum mâi mii kŏng |
| none | มึนเมา | mun-mao |
| there's none | ไม่มี | mâi mii |
| left | ไม่มีอะไรเหลือ | mâi mia-rai-lüa |
| non-smoking | ห้ามสูบบุหรี่ | hâam sùub-bu-rìi |
| north | เหนือ | nŭa |
| Northern Ireland | เกาะไอร์แลนด์เหนือ | gòe ai-laen nŭa |
| nose | จมูก | jà-mùuk |
| not | ไม่ | mâi |
| notebook | โน้ตบุ๊ก | note-book |
| nothing | ไม่มีอะไร | mâi mia-rai |

| English | Thai | Pronunciation |
|---|---|---|
| November | พฤศจิกายน | prút-sà-ji-gaa-yon |
| now | ตอนนี้ | dtom níi |
| number | ตัวเลข | dtua lêek |
| phone number | หมายเลขโทรศัพท์ | măai lêek too-rá-sàp |
| number plate | หมายเลขทะเบียน | măai lêek tà-bian |
| nurse | พยาบาล | pa-yaa-baan |
| nuts (bar nibbles) | ถั่ว | tùa |
| **O** | | |
| October | ตุลาคม | dtu-laa-kom |
| octopus | ปลาหมึกยักษ์ | bplaa-mùk-yák |
| off (radio, engine) | ปิด | bpìd |
| this is off (milk, food) | มันเสีย | man sĭa |
| office | สำนักงาน | săm-nák-ngaan |
| often | บ่อย | bòi |
| oil | น้ำมัน | náam-man |
| OK | ตกลง | dtòk-long |

| | | |
|---|---|---|
| old | แก่ | gàe |
| how old is it? | มันอายุกี่ | man aa-yú kìi |
| I'm ... years old... | ฉันอายุ ... ปี | chan aa-yú ... bpii |
| (building, etc.) | ... | bpii? |
| olives | มะกอก | mà-gòrk |
| olive oil | น้ำมันมะกอก | náam-man mà-gòrk |
| on | บน | bon |
| once | see GRAMMAR | |
| at once | ครั้งหนึ่ง | kráng nùng |
| one | ทันที | tan-tii |
| onion | หนึ่ง | nùng |
| only | หัวหอมใหญ่ | hùa-hǒm-yài |
| only one | เท่านั้น | tâo nán |
| | หนึ่งเดียวเท่า | nùng diao tǎo |
| | นั้น | nán |
| open | เปิด | bpèrd |
| is it open? | มันเปิด หรือเปล่า | man bpèrd rúu bplàao? |
| to open | เปิด | bpèrd |

| opening hours | ชั่วโมงทำการ | chûa-moong tam-gaan |
|---|---|---|
| opposite | ตรงข้าม | drong-kâam |
| optician | หมอตา | mǒr dtaa |
| or | หรือ | rǔu |
| orange (colour) | สีส้ม | sìi sôm |
| orange | ส้ม | sôm |
| orange juice | น้ำส้ม | náam-sôm |
| to order (food) | สั่งอาหาร | sàng aa-hǎan |
| other | อันอื่น | uun ùun |
| our | ของเรา | kǒng rao |
| out | ออก | òrk |
| out of order | ใช้การไม่ได้ | chái gaan mâi dâai |
| oven | เตาอบ | dtao-òp |
| to overtake | แซง | saeng |
| to owe | ติดหนี้ | dtìd-nîi |
| you owe me... | คุณติดหนี้ฉัน... | Khun dtìd-nîi chan... |
| owner | เจ้าของ | jâo-kǒng |

English – Thai

# English – Thai

## P

|  |  | |  |  | |
|---|---|---|---|---|---|
| to pack (bags) | เก็บของใส่กระเป๋า | gèb kŏng sài grà-bpǎo | to park | จอด | jòt |
| package tour | ทัวร์โปรแกรมท่องเที่ยว | chút bproo-graem tông-tîoa | partner (business) | หุ้นส่วน | hûn-sùan |
| packet | กระเป๋า | grà-bpǎo | *my partner* (couple) | คู่ชีวิตของฉัน | kôu-chii-wit |
| paid | จ่าย | jàai | party (celebration) | ปาร์ตี้ | kông chan |
| painful | เจ็บปวด | jèb bpùat | | | bpaa-tîi |
| *it's very painful* | มันปวดมาก | man bpùat mâak | passenger | ผู้โดยสาร | pûu-duoy-sǎan |
| painkiller | ยาแก้ปวด | yaa-gâe-bpùat | passport | หนังสือเดินทาง | nǎng-sǔu-dum-taang |
| painting (picture) | ภาพวาด | pâap-wâad | pasta | พาสต้า | pas-tâa |
| pair | คู่ | kûu | to pay | จ่าย | jàai |
| palace | วัง | wang | peanuts | ถั่ว | tùa |
| pancake | แพนเค้ก | paen-cake | pearl | ไข่มุก | kài-múk |
| paper | กระดาษ | grà-dàat | pedestrian | คนเดินเท้า | kon durn táao |
| *pardon!* | ขอโทษครับ/ค่ะ | kŏr-tôot krab/kà! | pedestrian crossing | ทางข้าม | taang-kâam |
| parents | พ่อแม่ผู้ปกครอง | pûu-bpòk-krong | pen | ปากกา | bpàak-gaa |
| park | สวน | sŭan | pencil | ดินสอ | din-sŏr |
| | | | penicillin | เพนนิซิลลิน | pen-ni-si-lin |

| English | Thai | Pronunciation |
|---|---|---|
| pepper (spice) | พริกไทย | prík-tai |
| per | ต่อ | dtòr |
| per hour | ต่อชั่วโมง | dtòr chûa-moong |
| per week | ต่ออาทิตย์ | dtòr aa-tít |
| per kilometre | ต่อกิโลเมตร | dtòr gi-loo-met |
| perfect | สมบูรณ์แบบ | sŏm-buun-bàep |
| it's perfect | มันสมบูรณ์แบบ | man sŏm-buun-bàep |
| performance | การแสดง | gaan sa-daeng |
| perfume | น้ำหอม | náam hŏm |
| permit | อนุญาต | à-nú-yâat |
| person | บุคคล | bùk-kon |
| per person | ต่อคน | dtòr kon |
| petrol | น้ำมันรถ | náam-man rót |
| petrol station | ปั๊มน้ำมัน | bpám náam man |
| phone | โทรศัพท์ | too-rá-sàp |
| phonecard | บัตรโทรศัพท์ | bàt too-rá-sàp |
| photocopy | ใบสำเนา | bai: sǎm-nao |
| photograph | ภาพถ่าย | pâap-tâai |
| picnic | ปิกนิก | bpìc-nìc |

| English | Thai | Pronunciation |
|---|---|---|
| picture (on wall) | ภาพ | pâap |
| pie | พาย | paai |
| piece (slice) | ชิ้น | chín |
| pill | ยา | yaa |
| pillow | หมอน | mŏrn |
| pin | เข็ม | kĕm |
| pink | สีชมพู | sĭi-chom-puu |
| pipe (for smoking) | กล้องสูบยา | glôrng sùub yaa |
| pipe (drain, etc.) | ท่อน้ำ | tôr náam |
| plain | ที่ราบ | tîi-râap |
| plane | เครื่องบิน | krûang bin |
| plastic | พลาสติก | plaas-tìk |
| plate | จาน | jaan |
| platform (railway) | ชานชาลา | chaan-chaa-laa |
| to play | เล่น | lên |
| please | กรุณา | ga-ru-naa |
| plug (electric) | ปลั๊ก | bplák |
| plumber | ช่างประปา | châang bprà-bpaa |
| pocket | กระเป๋าเสื้อ | grà-bpǎo sûa |
| poisonous | เป็นพิษ | bpen pít |

English – Thai

# English – Thai

| police | ตำรวจ | dtam-rùat | pot (for cooking) | หม้อ | môr |
| police station | สถานีตำรวจ | sa-tăa-nii dtam-rùat | potato | มันฝรั่ง | man-fà-ràng |
| | | | boiled potatoes | มันฝรั่งต้ม | man-fà-ràng-dtôm |
| polish (for shoes) | ขัด | kàd | fried potatoes | มันฝรั่งทอด | man-fà-ràng-tort |
| pool | สระน้ำ | sà-nám | | | |
| is there a pool? | มีสระน้ำไหม | mii sà-nám mái? | mashed potato | มันฝรั่งบด | man-fà-ràng-bòd |
| poor (not rich) | จน | jon | potato salad | สลัดมันฝรั่ง | sà-làd man-fà-ràng |
| pork | เนื้อหมู | núa-mŭu | | | |
| port (harbour) | ท่าเรือ | tâa ruua | powdered milk | นมผง | nom-pŏng |
| possible | เป็นไปได้ | bpen bpai dâai | prawns | กุ้งใหญ่ | gûng-yài |
| to post | ส่งทาง | sòng taang | to prefer | ปรารถนา | bpràad-ta-năa |
| | ไปรษณีย์ | bprai-sa-nii | I'd prefer tea | ฉันต้องการชา | chan dtông gaan chaa |
| postbox | ตู้ไปรษณีย์ | tûu-bprai-sa-nii | | | |
| postcard | ไปรษณียบัตร | bprai-sa-nii-ya-bàt | I'm pregnant | ท้อง | tóng |
| | | | pregnant | ตั้งครรภ์ | chan tóng |
| postcode | รหัสไปรษณีย์ | rà-hàt bprai-sa-nii | prescription | ใบสั่งยา | bai-sàng yaa |
| | | | present (gift) | ของขวัญ | kŏng-kwăn |
| poster | โปสเตอร์ | pos-sà-dtur | this is a present | นี่คือของขวัญ | nîi kuu kŏng-kwăn |
| post office | ที่ทำการ | tîi tam gaan | pretty | น่ารัก | nâa-rák |
| | ไปรษณีย์ | bprai-sa-nii | | | |

| | | |
|---|---|---|
| price | ราคา | raa-kaa |
| price list | ใบราคา | bai raa-kaa |
| private | ส่วนบุคคล | sùan bùk-kon |
| bathroom | ห้องน้ำส่วน | hông náam |
| private | ตัว | sùan-dtua |
| probably | คงจะ | kong jà |
| to pronounce | การออกเสียง | gaan òrk sĭang |
| public holiday | วันหยุดทั่วไป | wan yùt tûa-bpai |
| pudding | พุดดิ้ง | púd-dîng |
| to pull | ดึง | dung |
| purple | สีม่วง | sĭi mûang |
| pushchair | รถเข็น | rót kĕn |
| pyjamas | ชุดนอน | chút norn |

**Q**

| | | |
|---|---|---|
| quality | คุณภาพ | kun-ná-pâap |
| good quality | คุณภาพดี | kun-ná-pâap dii |
| poor quality | คุณภาพไม่ดี | kun-ná-pâap mâi dii |

| | | |
|---|---|---|
| queen | ราชินี | raa-chí-nii |
| question | คำถาม | kam-tăam |
| queue | คิว | kiu |
| to queue | เข้าคิว | kâo kiu |
| quickly | อย่างเร็ว | yàang reo |
| quiet | เงียบ | ngîap |
| quilt | ผ้านวม | pâa-nuaam |

**R**

| | | |
|---|---|---|
| rabbit (animal) | กระต่าย | grà-dtàai |
| rabies | โรคกลัวน้ำ | rôok-glua-náam |
| race (sport) | แข่ง | kàeng |
| radio | วิทยุ | wít-ta-yú |
| radish | หัวผักกาด | hŭa pàk-gàad |
| rain | ฝน | fŏn |
| raincoat | เสื้อกันฝน | sûa gan fŏn |
| raisins | ลูกเกด | lôuk gèet |
| rare (steak) | ดิบ | dìp |
| rash (skin) | ผื่น | pùun |
| rat | หนู | nŭu |

| rate | อัตรา | àt-dtraa |
| raw ham | แฮมดิบ | ham dìb |
| razor | มีดโกน | mîit-goon |
| to read (book, etc.) | อ่าน | àan |
| ready | พร้อม | próm |
| *is it ready?* | มันพร้อม หรือยัง? | man próm rǔu yang? |
| real | จริง, แท้ | jing, tàe |
| receipt | ใบเสร็จ | bai-sèt |
| reception (desk) | แผนกต้อนรับ | pa-nàek-ngaan dtô:n-ráp |
| recipe | ผู้ตรวจอาหาร | sùut aa-hǎan |
| to recommend | แนะนำ | náe-nam |
| red | สีแดง | sǐi daeng |
| *red wine* | ไวน์แดง | wine-daeng |
| reduction | การลดลง | gaan lót long |
| to refund | คืนเงิน | kuun ngum |
| regulations | ระเบียบข้อบังคับ | ra-bìap kôr bang-káp |

| relation (family member) | ความสัมพันธ์ | kwaam sǎm-pan |
| reliable (person, service) | เชื่อถือได้ | chûa tǔu dâai |
| to remember | จำ | jam |
| rent | เช่า | châo |
| to rent | การเช่า | gaan châo |
| to repair | การซ่อม | gaan sôm |
| to repeat | การทำซ้ำ | gaan tam sám |
| reservation | การจอง | gaan jo:ng |
| to reserve (room, table, etc.) | จอง | jo:ng |
| reserved | จองแล้ว | jo:ng láew |
| to rest | พักผ่อน | pák-pò:n |
| restaurant | ห้องอาหาร | hô:ng aa-hǎan |
| retired | เกษียณ | ga-sǐan |
| to return | กลับ | glàp |
| return (ticket) | ตั๋วกลับ | dtǔa glàp |
| reverse-charge call | เก็บเงินปลายทาง | gèb ngum bpaai taang |

| | | |
|---|---|---|
| rice (cooked) | ข้าวสวย | kâao sǔay |
| rich (person) | รวย | ruai |
| right (correct) | ถูกต้อง | tùuk dtô:ng |
| on/to the right | อยู่/ไปทางขวา | yùu/bpai taang kwǎa |
| ring (for finger) | แหวน | wǎen |
| river | แม่น้ำ | mâe náam |
| road | ถนน | tà-nǒn |
| road map | แผนที่ถนน | pǎen-tîi tà-nǒn |
| roof | หลังคา | lǎng-kaa |
| room | ห้อง | hô:ng |
| rope | เชือก | chûaok |
| rose | กุหลาบ | gù-làap |
| rotten (food) | เสีย | sǐa |
| route | เส้นทาง | sên-taang |
| rubber | ยาง | yaang |
| rug | พรม | prom |

## S

| | | |
|---|---|---|
| sad | เศร้า | sâo |
| safe | เซฟ | sép |
| safe (harmless) | ปลอดภัย | bplòrt-pai |
| safety pin | เข็มกลัด | kěm glàd |
| sailing | ออกเรือ | òrk ruaa |
| sale | ขาย | kǎai |
| for sale | สำหรับขาย | sǎm-ràp kǎai |
| salad | สลัด | sà-làd |
| salesperson | พนักงานขาย | pa-nák-ngaan kǎai |
| salmon | ปลาแซลมอน | bplaa sael-mo:n |
| salt | เกลือ | glua |
| same | เหมือน | mǔan |
| sand | ทราย | saai |
| sandals | รองเท้าแตะ | ro:ng-táao dtae |
| sardines | ปลาซาร์ดีน | bplaa-saa-diin |
| Saturday | วันเสาร์ | wan sǎo |
| sauce | น้ำจิ้ม | náam jîm |
| sausage | ไส้กรอก | sâi-gròrk |

# English – Thai

| English | Thai | Pronunciation | | English | Thai | Pronunciation |
|---|---|---|---|---|---|---|
| to say | พูด | pûud | | to sell | ขาย | kǎai |
| school | โรงเรียน | roong-rian | | to send | ส่ง | sòng |
| scissors | กรรไกร | gan-grai | | senior citizen | ผู้สูงอายุ | pûu sǔung aa-yú |
| Scotland | สก็อตแลนด์ | sà-gót-laen | | separate | แยก | yâek |
| Scottish | คนสก็อตแลนด์ | kon sà-gót-laen | | separately | แยกกัน | yâek gan |
| | | | | September | กันยายน | gan-yaa-yon |
| sculpture | งานปั้น | châang-bpân | | serious | จริงจัง | jing-jang |
| sea | ทะเล | tá-lee | | service | บริการ | bo:-ri-gaan |
| seafood | อาหารทะเล | aa-hǎan tá-lee | | service charge | ค่าบริการ | kâa bo:-ri-gaan |
| seasick | เมารือ | mao ruua | | shade (shadow) | ร่มเงา | rôm-ngao |
| I'm feeling | ฉันเมารือ | chan mao ruua | | shampoo | แชมพู | chaem-puu |
| seasick | | | | to shave | โกน | goon |
| seat (chair) | ที่นั่ง | tîi nâng | | shaver | ที่โกนหนวด | tîi goon nùat |
| reserved seat | จองที่นั่ง | joong tîi nâng | | shaving cream | ครีมโกน | kriim-goon-nùat |
| seat belt | เข็มขัดนิรภัย | kém-kàt ni-ra-pai | | | หนวด | |
| second | วินาที | winaa-tii | | she | เธอ | tur |
| second-class | ชั้นสอง | chán sǒ:ng | | sheet (for bed) | ผ้าปูเตียง | pâa– bpuu–dtiang |
| a second-class | ตั๋วชั้นสอง | dtǔa chán sǒ:ng | | shelf | ชั้น | chán |
| ticket | | | | shell | เปลือกหอย | bplùak-hǒ:i |
| secondhand | ของมือสอง | kǒ:ng muu sǒ:ng | | | | |

| English | Thai | |
|---|---|---|
| shellfish | หอย | hŏi |
| I don't eat shellfish | ฉันไม่กินหอย | chan mâi gin hŏi |
| ship | เรือ | ruua |
| shirt | เสื้อ | sûa |
| shoes | รองเท้า | ro:ng-táao |
| shop | ร้าน | ráan |
| shop assistant | พนักงานขาย | pa-nák-ngaan kăai |
| shopping | การเดินซื้อ | gaan dum súu |
| short | สั้น | sân |
| shorts (short trousers) | กางเกงขาสั้น | gaang-geeng-kăa-sân |
| show | แสดง | sa-daeng |
| to show | การแสดง | gaan sa-daeng |
| shower (bath) | ฝักบัว | fàk bua |
| shrimps | กุ้ง | gûng |
| shut | ปิด | bpìd |
| to shut | การปิด | gaan bpìd |

| English | Thai | |
|---|---|---|
| sick | ป่วย | bpài |
| I feel sick | ฉันรู้สึก คลื่นไส้ | chan rúu-sùk klûun-sâi |
| sign (road, notice, cheque, etc.) | ป้าย | bpài |
| to sign (form, cheque, etc.) | เซ็นชื่อ | sen chúu |
| signature | ลายเซ็น | laai-sen |
| silk | ไหม | mái |
| silver | เงิน | ngun |
| simple | ธรรมดา | tam-mà-daa |
| single (lone) | โสด | sòod |
| single (unmarried) | ยังไม่แต่งงาน | yang mái dtàeng-ngaan |
| I'm single | ฉันเป็นคน โสด | chan bpen kon sòod |
| single room | ห้องเดี่ยว | hông diao |
| sink | อ่างล้างจาน | àang láang jaan |
| sister (elder/younger) | พี่สาว/ น้องสาว | pii-sáao / nó:ng-sáao |
| sit | นั่ง | nâng |

| English | Thai | |
|---|---|---|
| size (shoes) | ขนาด | kà-nàat |
| *bigger size* | ขนาดใหญ่ | kà-nàat yài |
| *smaller size* | ขนาดเล็ก | kà-nàat lék |
| to skate | เล่นสเก็ต | lên sà-gét |
| skates | สเก็ต | sà-gét |
| skimmed milk | นมพร่องมันเนย | nom prô:ng man neei |
| skin | ผิว | piu |
| skirt | กระโปรง | gra-broong |
| sky | ท้องฟ้า | tórng fáa |
| to sleep | นอน | norn |
| sleeping bag | ถุงนอน | tǔng norn |
| sleeping pill | ยานอนหลับ | yaa-norn-làp |
| slice | ชิ้น | chín |
| slippers | รองเท้าแตะ | rorng-táao dtàe |
| slow | ช้า | cháa |
| small | เล็ก | lék |
| smaller | เล็กกว่า | lék gwàa |
| smell | กลิ่น | glìn |
| to smell | ได้กลิ่น | dâai glìn |

| English | Thai | |
|---|---|---|
| smile | ยิ้ม | yím |
| smoke | ควัน | kwan |
| to smoke | สูบบุหรี่ | sùub burìi |
| snake | งู | nguu |
| soap | สบู่ | sà-bùu |
| socks | ถุงเท้า | tǔng-táao |
| soft | นิ่ม | nîm |
| soft drink | เครื่องดื่ม | krûang duum |
| sold out | ขายออก | kǎai òk |
| someone | บางคน | baang kon |
| something | บางอย่าง | baang yàang |
| sometimes | บางเวลา | baang wee-laa |
| son | ลูกชาย | lûuk-chaai |
| song | เพลง | pleeng |
| soon | เร็วเร็วนี้ | reo reo níi |
| sorry: | | |
| *I'm sorry!* | ขอโทษครับ/<br>ค่ะ | kǒr-tôot krráp/ká |
| sort (type) | ชนิด | cha-nít |

| English | Thai | |
|---|---|---|
| soup | น้ำแกง | náam-gaeng |
| south | ใต้ | dtâi |
| souvenir | ของฝาก | kǒng-fàak |
| souvenir shop | ร้านขายของฝาก | ráan-kǎai-kǒng-fàak |
| to speak | พูด | pûud |
| special | พิเศษ | pi-sèet |
| speed | ความเร็ว | kwaam-reo |
| spell | สะกด | sà-kòt |
| spicy | เผ็ด | pèt |
| sponge (for cleaning) | ฟองน้ำ | fong-náam |
| spoon | ช้อน | chón |
| sport | กีฬา | gii-laa |
| squid | ปลาหมึกตัวเล็ก | bplaa-mùk-dtua-lék |
| stadium | สนามกีฬา | sà-nǎam-gii-laa |
| stairs | บันได | ban-dai |
| stamp | แสตมป์ | sà-dtaem |
| star | ดาว | daao |

| English | Thai | |
|---|---|---|
| to start | เริ่ม | rûrm |
| station | สถานี | sà-tǎa-nii |
| bus station | สถานีรถโดยสาร | sà-tǎa-nii-kǒn |
| | | sǒng |
| railway station | สถานีรถไฟ | sà-tǎa-nii rót fai |
| to stay | พัก | pák |
| still (not fizzy) | ไม่ซ่า, ไม่มีฟอง | mâi-sâa, |
| | | mâi mii fong |
| stomach | ท้อง | tóng |
| stop! | หยุด | yùd! |
| storm | พายุ | paa-yú |
| straight on (for drinking) | ตรงไป | dtrong bpai |
| straw | หลอด | lòrt |
| street | ถนน | tà-nǒn |
| street map | แผนที่ถนน | pǎen-tîi tà-nǒn |
| string | ด้าย | dâai |
| strong (tea, coffee) | เข้ม | kêm |

# English - Thai

| English | Thai | Pronunciation |
|---|---|---|
| stuck: | ติด | dtìd |
| it's stuck | มันติด | man dtìd |
| student | เด็กนักเรียน | dèk nák rian |
| stupid | โง่ | ngôo |
| sugar | น้ำตาล | náam dtaan |
| suit (clothes) | ชุด | sùut |
| suitcase | กระเป๋าเสื้อผ้า | grà-bpǎo sûa-pâa |
| summer | หน้าร้อน | nâa rórn |
| in summer | ในหน้าร้อน | nai nâa rórn |
| sun | พระอาทิตย์ | prá aa-tít |
| sunbathe | อาบแดด | àap dàet |
| sunburn | ผิวไหม้แดด | pǐu-mâi-dàet |
| Sunday | วันอาทิตย์ | wan aa-tít |
| sunglasses | แว่นกันแดด | wâen-gan-dàet |
| sunshade | ที่บังแดด | tîi-bang-dàet |
| suntan lotion | ครีมกันแดด | krim-gan-dàet |
| supermarket | ซูเปอร์มาร์เก็ต | sup-bpur-maa-gét |
| supplement | เสริม | sěrm |
| surfboard | กระดานโต้ | grà-daan-dtôo |
| surfing | โต้คลื่น | dtôo klûun |
| surname | นามสกุล | naam-sà-kun |
| sweater | เสื้อกันหนาว | sûa-gan-nǎao |
| sweet | หวาน | wǎan |
| sweetener | น้ำตาลเทียม | náam dtaan tiam |
| sweets | ของหวาน | kǒng-wǎan |
| to swim | ว่ายน้ำ | wâai-náam |
| swimming-pool | สระว่ายน้ำ | sà wâai-náam |
| swimsuit | ชุดว่ายน้ำ | chút wâai-náam |
| switch | สวิตช์ | sà-wìt |
| to switch off | ปิด | bpìd |
| to switch on | เปิด | bpèrd |
| swollen (finger, ankle, etc.) | บวม | buam |
| T | | |
| table | โต๊ะ | dtó |
| table tennis | ปิงปอง | bping-bpong |

| | | |
|---|---|---|
| to take | กาน | tàai |
| to talk | คุม | kui |
| tall | สูง | sŭung |
| tap | เทป | tép |
| tape (cassette) | เทปคาสเซ็ตต์ | tép-ka-sèt |
| taste | รสชาติ | rót-châat |
| tasty | อร่อย | aròy |
| tax | ภาษี | paa-sĭi |
| taxi | แท็กซี่ | táek-sîi |
| tea | น้ำชา | náam-chaa |
| teacher | ครู | kruu |
| team (football, etc) | ทีม | tiim |
| teeth | ฟัน | fan |
| telephone | โทรศัพท์ | too-rá-sàp |
| to telephone | โทร | too |
| telephone box | ตู้โทรศัพท์ | dtûu too-rá-sàp |
| telephone call | สายโทรศัพท์หมาย | mii too-rá-sàp |
| | มาย | maa |

| | | |
|---|---|---|
| international call | โทรต่าง ประเทศ | too dtàang-bpra- têet |
| | ส่งต่อโทรศัพท์ | sà-mùt too-rá- sàp |
| telephone directory | | |
| television | โทรทัศน์ | too-rá-tát |
| temperature | อุณหภูมิ | un-hà-puum |
| I have a temperature | ฉันตัวร้อน | chan dtua rórn |
| temporary | ชั่วคราว | chûa-kraao |
| tennis | เทนนิส | ten-nís |
| tennis ball | ลูกเทนนิส | lûuk ten-nís |
| tennis court | สนามเทนนิส | sà-nǎam ten-nís |
| tennis racket | ไม้เทนนิส | máai ten-nís |
| tent | เต็นท์ | dtén |
| terrace | ระเบียง | rá-biang |
| tetanus | โรคบาดทะยัก | rôok-bàat-ta-yák |
| thank you | ขอบคุณครับ / | kòrb kun krab/ká |
| | ขอบคุณค่ะ | |
| thanks | ขอบใจ | kòrb jai |
| that | นั้น | nán |

English – Thai

# English – Thai

| English | Thai | Transliteration |
|---|---|---|
| theatre | โรงละคร | roong-la-korn |
| there: | ที่นั่น | tîi nân |
| there is.../ there are... | มี ... | mii ... |
| is there...? | มี ... ... ไหม? | mii ... mái? |
| these | เหล่านี้ | lâo-nîi |
| they | พวกเขา | pûag-kăo |
| thief | ขโมย | kà-mooi |
| thin | ผอม | pörm |
| to think | คิด | kid |
| I think so | ฉันเห็นด้วย | chan hĕn dûoy |
| I don't think so | ฉันไม่เห็นด้วย | chan mâi hĕn dûoy |
| thirsty: | หิว (น้ำ), กระหาย | hiu (náam), gra-hǎai |
| I'm thirsty | ฉันหิวน้ำนี้ | chan hiu nám níi |
| this | นี้ | níi |
| those | เหล่านั้น | lâo-nán |
| thread | ด้าย | dâai |

| English | Thai | Transliteration |
|---|---|---|
| Thursday | วันพฤหัสบดี | wan-pá-rú-hàt-sa-bo-dii |
| ticket | ตั๋ว | dtŭa |
| single ticket | ตั๋วเที่ยวเดียว | dtŭa tîao diao |
| return ticket | ตั๋วไปกลับ | dtŭa bpai glàb |
| ticket office | ที่ขายตั๋ว | tîi kăai dtŭa |
| tie | เนคไท | neck-tai |
| tight | คับ | káb |
| it's too tight | มันคับเกินไป | man káb gun bpai |
| time | เวลา | wee-laa |
| timetable | ตารางเวลา | dtaa-raang wee-laa |
| tip (to waiter, etc.) | ทิป | tip |
| tired | เหนื่อย | nùai |
| tissues | ทิชชู่ | tít-chûu |
| to | ไป | bpai tîi |
| | | see GRAMMAR |
| to the station | ไปที่สถานี | bpai tîi sà-tăa-nii |
| toast | ปิ้ง | bpîng |
| today | วันนี้ | wan níi |

| English | Thai | |
|---|---|---|
| together | ด้วยกัน | dûoy-gan |
| toilet | ห้องสุขา | hông su-kâa |
| toilet paper | กระดาษชำระ | gra-dàat cham-rá |
| toll (on motorway) | ทางด่วน | taang dùan |
| tomato | มะเขือเทศ | má-kûa-têet |
| tomato juice | น้ำมะเขือเทศ | náam má-kûa-têet |
| tomato salad | สลัดมะเขือเทศ | sà-làd má-kûa-têet |
| tomorrow | พรุ่งนี้ | prûng níi |
| tomorrow evening | เย็นพรุ่งนี้ | yen prûng níi |
| tomorrow morning | พรุ่งนี้เช้า | prûng níi cháao |
| tonight | คืนนี้ | kuun níi |
| tooth | ฟัน | fan |
| toothache | ปวดฟัน | bpùat-fan |
| toothbrush | แปรงสีฟัน | bpraeng sǐi-fan |
| toothpaste | ยาสีฟัน | yaa-sǐi-fan |
| total | รวมทั้งหมด | ruam táng-mòt |

| English | Thai | |
|---|---|---|
| tough (meat) | เหนียว | nǐao |
| tour | ทัวร์ | tuaa |
| tourist | นักท่องเที่ยว | nák-tông-tîao |
| tourist office | สำนักงานบริการนักท่องเที่ยว | sǔun bo-ri-gaan nák-tông-tîao |
| towel (hand towel) | ผ้าเช็ดมือ | pâa chét muu |
| towel | ผ้าเช็ดตัว | pâa chét dtua |
| town | เมือง | muang |
| town hall | ศาลากลาง | sǎa-laa glaang |
| toy | ของเล่น | kǒng lên |
| traditional | ตามประเพณีดั้งเดิม | dtaam bpràa-pee-nii |
| traffic | จราจร | ja-raa-jorn |
| traffic lights | ไฟจราจร | fai ja-raa-jorn |
| train | รถไฟ | rót-fai |
| to translate | แปล | bplae |
| to travel | ท่องเที่ยว | tông-tîao |
| travel agent | บริษัททัวร์เที่ยว | bò-ri-sàt tông-tîao |

English – Thai

# English – Thai

| travellers' cheques | เช็คเดินทาง | check-dœm taang |
| tree | ต้นไม้ | dtôn-máai |
| trip | การเดินทาง | gaan dœm taang |
| trousers | กางเกงขายาว | gaang-geeng-kǎa-yao |
| truck | รถบรรทุก | rót-ban-túk |
| true | จริง | jing |
| that's true | มันจริง | man jing |
| that's not true | มันไม่จริง | man mâi jing |
| try on | ลองใส่ | long sài |
| t-shirt | เสื้อยืด | sûa yûud |
| Tuesday | วันอังคาร | wan ang-kaan |
| tuna | ปลาทูน่า | bplaa-tuu-nâa |
| tunnel | อุโมงค์ | ù-moong |
| to turn off (radio, light) | ปิด | bpìd |
| to turn on | เปิด | bpùrd |
| tweezers | คีมหนีบ | kiim-nìip |
| twins | ฝาแฝด | fǎa-fàet |

## U

| ugly | น่าเกลียด | nâa-glìat |
| umbrella | ร่ม | rôm |
| uncle (paternal) | ลุง | aa |
| uncle (maternal) | น้า | náa |
| uncomfortable | ไม่สะดวก | mâi-sà-duak |
| underground (metro) | รถไฟใต้ดิน | rót fai dtâi din |
| understand | เข้าใจ | kâo jai |
| I don't understand | ฉันไม่เข้าใจ | chan mâi kâo jai |
| do you understand? | คุณเข้าใจไหม | kun kâo jai mǎi? |
| underwear | ชุดชั้นใน | chút chán nai |
| unemployed | ว่างงาน | wâang ngaan |
| university | มหาวิทยาลัย | mà-hǎa-wít-ta-yaa-lai |
| unlucky | โชคร้าย | chôok-ráai |
| upstairs | ชั้นบน | chán bon |
| urgent | ด่วน | dùan |

| English | Thai | |
|---|---|---|
| it's urgent | มีเหตุด่วน | man dûan |
| to use | ใช้ | chái |
| useful | มีประโยชน์ | mii-bprà-yòot |
| usually | ปกติ | bpòk-gà-dti |
| **V** | | |
| vacancy (room) | ห้องว่าง | hông-wâang |
| vacuum cleaner | เครื่องดูดฝุ่น | krûang dùut fun |
| valid | ใช้ได้ | mâi mòt aa-yú |
| valuable | มีค่า | mii-kâa |
| van | รถตู้ | rót dtûu |
| VAT | ภาษีมูลค่าเพิ่ม | paa-sǐi muun-la-kâa-pêrm |
| veal | เนื้อลูกวัว | núa lûuk wua |
| vegetable | ผัก | pàk |
| vegetarian | มังสวิรัติ | mang sà-vi-rát |
| very | มาก | mâak |
| very good | ดีมาก | dii mâak |
| view | ดู | duu |

| English | Thai | |
|---|---|---|
| village | หมู่บ้าน | mùu-bâan |
| visa | วีซ่า | vii-sâa |
| to visit | เยี่ยม | yîam |
| visitor | ผู้มาเยี่ยม | pûu maa yîam |
| vitamin pills | วิตามิน | vit-ta-min |
| volleyball | วอลเลย์บอล | voi-lêe-bon |
| **W** | | |
| to wait (for) | รอ | ror |
| *please wait* | กรุณารอด้วย | ka-ru-naa ror pôm dûay |
| waiter/waitress | พนักงานเสิร์ฟ | pa-nák-ngaan sûrp |
| waiting room | ห้องนั่งรอ | hông nâng ror |
| to wake up | ตื่น | dtùun |
| walk | เดิน | dum |
| to walk | เดิน | dum |
| walking-stick | ไม้เท้า | máai táao |
| wallet | กระเป๋าเงิน | grà-bpào ngum |
| to want | ต้องการ | dtô:ng gaan |

**English – Thai**

# English – Thai

| English | Thai | |
|---|---|---|
| war | สงคราม | sŏng-kraam |
| wardrobe | ตู้เสื้อผ้า | dtûu sûa-pâa |
| warm | อุ่น | ùn |
| to wash | ล้าง | láang |
| washbasin | อ่างล้างหน้า | àang láang nâa |
| washing machine | เครื่องซักผ้า | krûeang sák pâa |
| washing powder | น้ำยาซักผ้า | náam yaa sák pâa |
| wasp | ตัวต่อ | dtua dtòr |
| watch (wrist) | นาฬิกาข้อมือ | naa-lí-gaa kôr muu |
| water | น้ำ | náam |
| distilled water | น้ำกลั่น | náam glàn |
| mineral water | น้ำแร่ | náam râe |
| fresh water | น้ำสะอาด | náam sà-àat |
| waterfall | น้ำตก | náam dtòk |
| waterproof | กันน้ำ | gan-náam |
| water-skiing | สกีน้ำ | sà-gii náam |
| wave | คลื่น | klûun |

| English | Thai | |
|---|---|---|
| way | ทาง | taang |
| is this the right way? | ตรงนี้ถูกทางไหม? | dtrong níi tùuk taang mái? |
| way out | ทางออก | taang òrk |
| we | เรา | rao |
| weak (tea, coffee, drink) | มั่นเข้มข้น | see GRAMMAR mâi kêm kôn |
| to wear | ใส่ | sài |
| weather forecast | พยากรณ์อากาศ | pá-yaa-gorn aa-gàat |
| wedding | งานแต่งงาน | ngaan dtàeng-ngaan |
| wedding ring | แหวนแต่งงาน | wăen dtàeng-ngaan |
| Wednesday | วันพุธ | wan pút |
| week | สัปดาห์ | sàp-daa |
| last week | สัปดาห์ที่แล้ว | sàp-daa tîi láew |
| next week | สัปดาห์หน้า | sàp-daa nâa |

|  |  | |  |  |
|---------|------|---|---------|------|
| weekend | วันหยุดเสาร์ อาทิตย์ | wan-yùd sǎo aa-tìt | whose: | ของใคร | kŏ:ng krai |
| weekly | ประจำสัปดาห์ | bpra-jam sàp-daa | whose is it? | มันเป็นของของ ใคร? | man bpen kŏ:ng krai? |
| weight | น้ำหนัก | náam-nàk | why | ทำไม | tam-mai |
| welcome! | ยินดีต้อนรับ! | Yindii dtô:n ráb! | wife | ภรรยา | panyaa |
| well | ดี | dii | window | หน้าต่าง | nâa-dtàang |
| well done (meat) | สุกสุก | sùk sùk | windy: | ลมแรง | lom raeng |
| wet | เปียก | bpìak | it's windy | ลมแรง | lom raeng |
| what | อะไร | a-rai | wine | ไวน์ | wine |
| what is it? | มันคืออะไร? | man kuu a-rai? | red wine | ไวน์แดง | wine-daeng |
| wheelchair | รถเข็น | rót kĕn | white wine | ไวน์ขาว | wine-kǎo |
| when? | เมื่อไหร่ | mûa-râi? | wine list | รายการไวน์ | raai gaan wine |
| where? | ที่ไหน | tîi nǎi? | with | ด้วย | dôuy |
| which? | อันไหน? | an nǎi? | without | ปราศจาก | bpràat-sa-jàak |
| which one? | อันไหน? | an nǎi? | | | see GRAMMAR |
| white | ขาว | kǎao | woman | ผู้หญิง | pûu-yǐng |
| who | ใคร | krai | wood (substance) | แผ่นไม้ | pàen máai |
| whole | ทั้งหมด | táng mòt | word | คำ | kam |
| | | | to work | ทำงาน | tam-ngaan |

English – Thai

# English – Thai

| | | |
|---|---|---|
| *it doesn't work* | มันไม่ทำงาน | man mâi tam-ngaan |
| **wrap** | ห่อ | hòr |
| *please wrap* | ช่วยห่อให้ | chûai hòr man |
| *it up* | ด้วยครับ / ค่ะ | dûoy krab/kà |
| to write | เขียน | kĭan |
| writing paper | กระดาษ | grà-dàat |
| wrong | ผิด | pìd |

## X

| | | |
|---|---|---|
| x-ray | เอ็กซ์เรย์ | ék-sà-ree |

## Y

| | | |
|---|---|---|
| yacht | เรือยอชต์ | ruua yórt |
| year | ปี | bpii |
| *this year* | ปีนี้ | bpii níi |
| yellow | สีเหลือง | sĭi lŭang |
| yes | ใช่ | châi |
| yesterday | เมื่อวาน | mûa-waan |
| you | คุณ | khun |

## Z

| | | |
|---|---|---|
| zero | ศูนย์ | sŭun |
| zip code | รหัสไปรษณีย์ | rá-hàt-prai-sa-nii |
| zoo | สวนสัตว์ | sŭan sàt |

# Thai – English

## ก

|  |  |  |
|------|-------------|---------|
| กระเป๋าใส่เงิน | grà-bpǎo kěm-kàt | money belt |
| การเข้าไป | gaan kâo bpai | to enter |
| กระเป๋าเสื้อ | grà-bpǎo sûa | pocket |
| กระดาษ | grà-dàat | paper |
| กระต่าย | grà-dtàai | rabbit (animal) |
| กรุณาอย่าสูบบุหรี่ | ga-ru-naa yàa sùub burìi | please don't smoke |
| กลับไป | glàb bpai | to go back |
| ก่อนอาหารค่ำ | gòn aa-hǎan kâm | before dinner |
| กางเกงขายาว | gaang-geeng-kǎa-yao | trousers |
| การหลบหนี | gaan lòp nǐi | escape |
| กุมภาพันธ์ | gum-paa-pan | February |
| เก็บเงินทอนไว้ครับ/ค่ะ | gèb ngurn torn wái krab/kâ | keep the change |
| เกาะ | gò | island |
| กรมท่า | grom-má-tâa | navy blue |
| กรรไกร | gan-grai | scissors |
| กระดาษชำระ | grà-dàat cham-rá | toilet paper |
| กรุณาอธิบาย | ka-ru-naa à-tí-baai | please explain |
| กล่อง | glòng | box |
| กลุ่ม | glùm | group (of people) |
| ก่อนหน้า | gòn nâa | before |
| ก่อนสี่โมง | gòn sìi moong | before 4 o'clock |
| กอล์ฟ | golf | golf |
| กาแฟเย็น | gaa-fae-yen | iced coffee |
| กาแฟสำเร็จรูป | gaa-fae sǎm-rèt-rûub | instant coffee |
| การจอง | gaan jorng | booking |
| การตัด | gaan dtàt | to cut |
| การประชุม | gaan bpra-chum | meeting |
| กิน | gin | to eat |
| กุ้ง | gûng | prawns |
| เก็บเงินด้วยครับ/คะ | gèb ngurn dûoy krab/kâ | the bill, please |
| เก็บเงินทอนไว้ครับ/ค่ะ | gèb ngurn torn wái krab/kâ | keep the change |

# Thai – English

|  |  |  |
|---|---|---|
| เกินพิกัดน้ำหนาก | gèb ngum bplaai | reverse-charge |
| ทาง | taang | call |
| เกมส์ | game | match (game) |
| เกลือ | glua | salt |
| เก็บ | gèb | to keep |
| เก้าอี้ | gâo-îi | chair |
| เก้าอี้ผ้าใบ | gâo-îi-pâa-bai | deck chair |
| เกาะไอร์แลนด์เหนือ | gò: ai-laen núa | Northern Ireland |
| แล้วคุณเกิด | gùrt kún | to happen |
| เกิดอะไรขึ้น | gùrt a-rai kún? | what happened? |
| แก๊ส | gá: | gas |
| กรกฎาคม | ga-rá-gà-daa-kom | July |
| กระเทียม | grà-tiam | garlic |
| กระเป๋า | grà-bpǎo | pocket |
| กระเป๋า | grà-bpǎo | bag |
| กระเป๋าเดินทาง | grà-bpǎo dum taang | baggage |

|  |  |  |
|---|---|---|
| กระเป๋าเดินทาง | grà-bpào dum taang | luggage |
| กระเป๋าเสื้อผ้า | grà-bpǎo sûa-pâa | suitcase |
| กระเป๋าถือ | grà-bpǎo tǔu | hand luggage |
| กระเป๋ามือถือ | grà-bpǎo muu tǔu | handbag |
| กระแสไฟ | grà-sǎe-fai | current |
| กระโปรงชุด | grà-bproong-chút | dress |
| กระจก | grà-jòk | mirror |
| กระจกส่องดูคลื่น | grà-daan-dtòo klûun | surfboard |
| กระดาษ | grà-dàat | writing paper |
| กระดูก | grà-dùuk | bone |
| กระป๋อง | grà-bpǒ:ng | can |
| กระปุก | grà-bpùk | jar |
| ก้ม | gôm | bend |
| กล้องถ่ายรูป | glô:ng tàai rûub | camera |
| กล้องถ่ายภาพหนัง | glô:ng tàai nǎng | camcorder |
| กลาง | glaang | middle |
| กลางคืน | glaang kuun | night |
| กอล์ฟคลับ | golf club | golf club |

| Thai | | English |
|---|---|---|
| กัด | gàt | bite (insect, dog) |
| กันน้ำ | gan-náam | waterproof |
| กาแฟ | gaa-fae | coffee |
| กาแฟไม่มีคา เฟอีน | gaa-fae mâi mii kaa-fee-in | decaffeinated coffee |
| กาแฟดำ | gaa-fae-dam | black coffee |
| กาแฟสำเร็จรูป | gaa-fae săm-rèt-rûub | instant coffee |
| กางเกงขายาว | gaang-geeng-kǎa-yao | pants (trousers) |
| กางเกงขาสั้น | gaang-geeng-kǎa-sân | shorts (shorts) |
| การเต้นรำ | gaan dtên-ram | dance |
| การเข้าไปในสู่ | gaan kâo bpai sùu | to get into |
| การเช่า | gaan châo | to rent |
| การดื้อซื้อ ของ | gaan dum súu kŏng | shopping |
| การเปิด | gaan bpòert | open |
| การแสดง | gaan sa-daeng | to show |
| การแสดง | gaan sa-daeng | performance |

| Thai | | English |
|---|---|---|
| การควบคุม อาหาร | gaan kûap-kum aa-hǎan | diet |
| การซ่อม | gaan sôm | to repair |
| การ์ด | gàat | card |
| การ์ดวันเกิด | gàat wan gùrt | birthday card |
| การดื่ม | gaan dùum | to drink |
| การบันเทิง | gaan ban-turng | entertainment |
| การบิน | gaan bin | fly |
| การปิด | gaan bpìd | to shut |
| การออกเสียง | gaan òrk sìang | pronunciation |
| การอาบน้ำ | gaan-àap-náam | bath |
| กีฬา | gii-laa | game (sport) |
| เกษียณ | gà-sĭan | retired |
| แก่ | gàe | old |
| กระเป๋าเงิน | grà-bpǎo ngun | wallet |
| กระโปรง | gra-proong | skirt |
| กรุณา | ga-ru-naa | please |
| กลิ่น | glìn | smell |
| กันยายน | gan-yaa-yon | September |
| การเชิญ | gaan chum | to invite |

| | | |
|---|---|---|
| การเดินทาง | gaan dum taang | trip |
| การเดินทาง | gaan dum taang | journey |
| การจอง | gaan jorng | reservation |
| การทำซ้ำ | gaan tam sám | to repeat |
| การลดลง | gaan lót long | reduction |
| กีฬา | gii-laa | sport |
| กุ้ง | gúng | shrimps |
| กุญแจ | gun-jae | key |
| กุหลาบ | gù-làap | rose |
| โกรธ | gròot | angry |
| แก้ว | gâew | glass (for drink) |
| ไกล | glai | far |
| ไกลไหม? | glai mái? | is it far? |
| โกโก้ | goo-gòo | cocoa |
| โกน | goon | to shave |
| ใกล้ | glâi | close |
| กุ | | |
| เข็ม | kém | pin |
| เข็มขัดนิรภัย | kém-kàt ni-rá-pai | seat belt |
| เข่า | kào | knee |

| | | |
|---|---|---|
| โจม | ka-mooi | thief |
| ข้อผิดพลาด | kòr pìd-plâat | mistake |
| ข้าง | kâang | beside; next to |
| เข็มขัดนิรภัย | kém-kàt ni-rá-pai | seat belt |
| เข็ม | kém | needle |
| เข็มขัด | kém-kàt | belt |
| เข้าคิว | káo queue | queue |
| เข้ามาแทน | káo màa taen | to replace |
| แขก | kàek | guest |
| ขอโทษครับ/ค่ะ | kŏr-tôot krab/kà! | excuse me! |
| ของขวัญ | kŏng-kwaan | gift |
| ของขวัญ | kŏng-kwaan | present (gift) |
| ของหวาน | kŏng-wǎan | sweets |
| ขอบใจ | kòrb jai | thanks |
| ข้างล่าง | kâang-lâang | below |
| ขาออก | kǎa òrk | departures |
| เข้ม | kém | strong (tea, coffee) |
| เข็มกลัด | kém glàd | safety pin |

**Thai – English**

เอิมเบกนาม - เครดิตการ์ด

| Thai | | English |
|---|---|---|
| เข็มกับด้าย | kěm gàb dâai | a needle and thread |
| เข็มทิศ | kěm-tít | compass |
| เขา | kǎo | he |
| เข้าใจ | kǎo jai | understand |
| เข้าไป | kǎo bpai | to go in |
| เข้ามา | kǎo-maa | come in! |
| เขียน | kian | to write |
| เขียว | kiao | green |
| แข่ง | kaeng | race (sport) |
| ขนาดเล็ก | kà-nàat lék | small size |
| ขม | kǒm | bitter (taste) |
| ขวด | kùat | bottle |
| ขอโทษ! | kǒr tôot! | pardon! |
| ขนมปัง | ka-nǒm bpang | bread |
| ขนาด | kà-nàat | size (shoes) |
| ขนาดใหญ่ | kà-nàat yài | bigger size |
| ขยะ | kà-yà | litter (rubbish) |
| ของใคร | kǒng krai | whose |
| ของฝาก | kǒng faak | souvenir |

| Thai | | English |
|---|---|---|
| ข้างหน้า | kang nar | front |
| ข้างหน้า | kǎang-nâa | straight ahead |
| ขาย | kǎai | to sell |
| ขาว | kǎao | white |
| ไข่ | kài | egg |
| ไข่มุก | kài-múk | pearl |
| ขอโทษครับ/ค่ะ! | kǒr tôot krab/kà! | I'm sorry! |
| ข้อความ | kôr-kwaam | message |
| ของเล่น | kǒng lên | toy |
| ของมือสอง | kǒng muu sǒ:ng | secondhand |
| ของหวาน | kǒng-wǎan | dessert |
| ขอบคุณครับ/ค่ะ | kòrb kun krab/kà | thank you |
| ขัด | kàd | polish (for shoes) |
| ข้อมูล | kôr-moon | information |
| ขับ | kàp | to drive |
| ขา | kǎa | leg |
| ขาเข้า | kǎa-kǎo | arrivals |
| ข้างบน | kǎang-bon | above |

|  |  |  |
|---|---|---|
| ข้างหน้า | kâang nâa | in front of |
| ข้างหลัง | kâang lǎng | behind |
| ขาย | kǎai | sale, for sale |
| ขายหมด | kǎai mòt | sold out |
| ข่าว | kàao | news |
| ข้าวสวย | kâao sǔay | rice (cooked) |
| ไข้หวัดใหญ่ | kâi-wàt-yài | flu |
| คงจะ | kongjà | probably |
| คนเดินเท้า | kon dun táao | pedestrian |
| คนขับ | kon kàp | driver |
| คนดูแลเด็ก | kon-duu-lae-dèk | baby-sitter |
| คนฝรั่งเศส | kon fà-ràng-sèet | French |
| คนพิการ | kon pí-gaan | disabled (person) |
| คนรับใช้ | kon ráp chái | maid |
| คนสก็อตแลนด์ | kon sà-gót-laen | Scottish |
| คนหา | kón-hǎa | to find |
| คนอังกฤษ | kon ang-grìt | English |
| ครอบครัว | krôp-krua | family |
| ครั้งแรก | kráng râek | first |
| ครีมกันแดด | kriim-gan-dàet | suntan lotion |
| ครีมนวดผม | kriim-nûat-pǒm | conditioner (for hair) |
| คีมหนีบ | kiim-nìp | tweezers |
| ครึ่งชั่วโมง | krûng chûa moong | half an hour |
| คลื่น | klûun | wave |
| ควัน | kwan | smoke |
| ความเร็ว | kwaam-reo | speed |
| ความดันเลือด | kwaam-dan lûat | blood pressure |
| ความดันสูง | kwaam-dan sǔung | high blood pressure |
| ความสนใจ | kwaam-sǒn-jai | attention |
| ความสัมพันธ์ | kwaam-sǎm-pan | relation (family member) |
| ความสูง | kwaam-sǔung | height |
| อันตราย | an-dta-raai | danger |
| คอนแทคเลนส์ | kon-tæk-len | contact lens |
| คอมพิวเตอร์ | com-pu-ter | computer |
| เครดิตการ์ด | kree-dìt-gàat | credit card |

# Thai – English

|  |  |  |
|---|---|---|
| เครื่องดื่มมึนเมา | krûang dùum mun-mao | alcohol |
| เค้ก | cake | cake |
| คริสต์มาส | krit-sa-mâat | Christmas |
| คนเยอรมัน | kon yur-rá-man | German |
| ครอบครัวฉัน | krôp-krua kŏng chan | my family |
| คอ | kor | neck |
| ค่าโดยสาร | kâa duoy-săan | fare (train, bus) |
| คุณสบายดี หรือ? | khun sà baai dii rúu? | how are you? |
| โค้ก | kók | Coke® |
| โคมไฟ | koom-fai | lamp |
| คนจับปลา | kon jàb bplaa | fisherman |
| คนต่างชาติ | kon dtàang-châat | foreigner |
| คนทำขนมปัง | kon tam ka-nŏm bpang | baker's |
| คนออสเตรเลีย | kon òt-sa-dtree-lia | Australian |
| คนอิตาลี | kon i-dtaa-li | Italian |
| ครีม | kriim | cream (dairy) |
| ครึ่ง | krûng | half |
| ครึ่งขวด | krûng kùat | half bottle |
| ครู | kruu | teacher |
| ความเร็ว | kwaam-reo | maximum |
| สูด | sǔung sùt | speed |
| ความถี่ | kwaam tii | frequency |
| ความร้อน | kwaam róm | heat |
| ความสะอาด | kwaam sà-àat | cleanliness |
| ความสุข | kwaam sùk | happiness |
| ฝ้าย, ผ้าฝ้าย | kót-dtôn, pâa fâai | cotton (material) |
| คอนเสิร์ต | kon-sùt | concert |
| ค่าเข้า | kâa kâo | entrance fee |
| ค่าธรรมเนียม | kâa-tam-niam | charge (fee) |
| คำ | kam | word |
| คำตอบ | kam-dtòrb | answer |
| คุณชื่ออะไร | khun chûu a-rai? | what's your name? |
| ใคร | krai | who |

220 | 221

## Thai – English

## Thai - English

|  |  |  |
|---|---|---|
| **ง** | | |
| เงิน | ngun | money |
| เงิน | ngun | silver |
| งาน | ngaan | job |
| งู | nguu | snake |
| เงินสด | ngun-sòt | cash |
| เงียบ | ngîap | quiet |
| งานแต่งงาน | ngaan dtaeng-ngaan | wedding |
| งาน | ngaan | wedding |
| **จ** | | |
| จบ | job | end |
| จำนวนเท่าไหร่ | jam-nuan tâo-rài? | how many? |
| จมน้ำ | jom náam | to drown |
| จมูก | ja-mùuk | nose |
| จราจร | ja-raa-jom | traffic |
| จอง | jo:ng | to queue to book |
| จองที่นั่ง | jo:ng tîi nâng | to reserve a seat |
| จด | jòrt | land |
| จักรยาน | jàk-grà-yaan | bicycle |
| จาก | jàak | to leave |
| จาก | jàak | from |
| จากไป | jàak bpai | go away |
| จ่าย | jàai | to pay |
| จำเป็น | jam-bpen | necessary |
| จูบ | jùup | to kiss |
| เจ็บ | jèb | hurt |
| เจ้าของ | jâo-kŏ:ng | owner |
| จน | jon | poor (not rich) |
| เจ็บปวด | jèb bpùat | painful |
| โจมตี / ประจัญบาน | joom-dtii (war)/ bpra-tút-sa-ráai | to attack (person) |
| ใจดี | jai dii | kind |
| คุณใจดีมาก | khun jai dii mâak | you're very kind |
| จำนวน | jam-nuan | amount |
| จ่าย | jàai | to pay |
| จาน | jaan | plate |
| จะซื้อ | jà súu | to buy |
| จอง | jo:ng | to reserve (room, table, etc.) |
| จองแล้ว | jo:ng láew | reserved |

|  |  |  |
| --- | --- | --- |
| จริงจังหรือ | jing-jang rʉ́u? | is it serious? |
| จริงจัง | jing-jang | serious |
| จริง | jing | true |
| จริง | jing | real |
| จู่โจม/กำกับ | jùu-joom/ gam-rúrp | attack |
| จำ | jam | to remember |
| จะบิน | jà bin | to fly |
| จอด | jòrt | to park |
| ฉันเจ็บมือ | chan jèb muu | my hand hurts |
| ฉันเป็นคนโสด | chan bpen kon sòod | I'm single |
| ฉันเป็นคนอังกฤษ | chan bpen kon ang-grìt | I'm English |
| ฉันเห็นด้วย | chan hèn dûoy | I think so |
| ฉันเหนื่อย | chan nûai | I feel tired |
| ฉันแต่งงานแล้ว | chan dtàeng-ngaan láew | I'm married |
| ฉันชื่อ | chan chûu | my name is |
| ฉัน | chan | I |
| ฉันไม่เข้าใจ | chan mâi kâo jai | I don't understand |
| ฉันท้อง | chan tóing | I'm pregnant |
| ฉันต้องการ | chan dtô.ng gaan | I need... |
| ฉันต้องไป | chan dtô.ng bpai | I need to go |
| ฉันชอบกาแฟ | chan chôrp gaa-fae | I like coffee |
| ฉันจองไว้แล้ว | chan jo.ng wai láew | I've booked |
| ฉันไม่ชอบกาแฟ | chan mâi chôrp gaa-fae | I don't like coffee |
| ฉันไม่เห็นด้วย | chan mâi hèn dûoy | I don't think so |
| ฉันโกรธ | chan gròot | I'm angry |
| ฉันเมา | chan mao | I'm drunk |
| ฉันเป็นหม้าย | chan bpen mâai | I'm divorced |
| ฉันเป็นโสด | chan bpen sòod | I'm not married |
| ฉันไม่เป็นอะไร | chan mâi bpen a-rai | I'm all right |

|  |  |  |
|---|---|---|
| จันไม่รู้ | chan mâi róo | I don't know |
| จันตัวร้อน | chan dtua rórn | I have a temperature |
| จันถ่ายภาพได้ไหม | chan tàai-pâap dâai mái | can I take pictures? |
| จันปวดหัว | chan bpùat hŭa | I've got a headache |
| จันป่วย | chan bpùai | I'm ill |
| จันรักคุณ | chan rák khun | I love you |
| เช็คอิน | check-in | to check in |
| ชน | chon | crash (collision) |
| ช็อกโกแล็ต | chók-goo-láet | chocolate |
| ชอบ | chôrp | enjoy |
| ชั้นบน | chán bon | upstairs |
| ชั้นสอง | chán sŏng | second-class |
| ชั้นหนึ่ง | chán nùng | first floor |
| ชั้นหนึ่ง | chán nùng | first class |
| ชั่วโมง | chûa-moong | hour |
| ชั่วโมงทำการ | chûa-moong tam gaan | opening hours |
| ชั่วคราว | chûa-kraao | temporary |
| ช้า | cháa | slow |
| ช่างทำผม | châang tam pŏm | hairdresser |
| ชานเมือง | chaan muang | suburb |
| ช่างปั้น | châang-bpân | sculpture |
| เช็ค | check | cheque |
| เช็คเดินทาง | chéck-dum-taang | travellers' cheques |
| เชอรี่ | chur-rîi | cherry |
| เช่า | chào | to hire |
| เช้านี้ | cháao níi | this morning |
| เชือก | chûak | rope |
| แช่แข็ง | châe-kǎeng | frozen |
| แชมเปญ | chaem-bpeen | champagne |
| แชมพู | chaem-puu | shampoo |
| โชคร้าย | chôok-ráai | unlucky |
| ใช่ | châi | yes |
| ใช้ | chái | to use |

|  | | |  | | |
|---|---|---|---|---|---|
| ไชโย | chai-yo | cheers! | ชุดว่ายน้ำ | chút wâai-náam | swimsuit |
| ชิ้น | chín | piece (slice) | ชีส | chees | cheese |
| ชุดโปรแกรมทัวร์ท่องเที่ยว | chút bproo-graem tô·ng-tîao | package tour | ชาวนา | chao naa | farmer |
| ชุดนอน | chút norn | pyjamas | ชายหาด | chaai-hàat | beach |
| เช่า | châo | rent | กาแฟดำเย็น | chaa-dam-yen | iced coffee |
| เชื่อถือได้ | chûa tûu dâi | reliable (person, service) | ช่างประปา | châang-bprà-bpaa | plumber |
| ชุดชั้นใน | chút chán nai | underwear | ช่างตัดผม | châang-dtàt-pǒm | barber |
| ชื่อ | chûu | name | ชาเย็น | chaa-yen | iced tea |
| ชิ้น | chín | slice | ชั้นล่าง | chán lâang | downstairs |
| ชานชาลาไหน | chaan-chaa-laa nái? | which platform? | ชั้น | chán | floor |
| ชานชาลา | chaan-chaa-laa | platform (railway) | ชอบ | chôrp | to like |
| ชั้น | chán | shelf | ช่องแช่เย็น | chô·ng-châe-yen | freezer |
| ช้อน | chón | spoon | ช่วยด้วย | chûai dûoy | help! |
| ช็อกโกแลตร้อน | chó·k-goo-láet rórn | hot chocolate | ช่วย | chûai | to help |
| สีชมพู | sǐi-chom-puu | pink | ช่วงบ่ายนี้ | chûang bàai níi | in the afternoon |
| ชนบท | chon-nà-bòt | country side | เช็ค | chéque | cheque |
| | | | เช้าเช้า | cháao cháo | early |
| | | | เชื่อ | chûa | to believe |
| | | | เชื้อเพลิง | chúa plumg | fuel |

## Thai – English

# Thai – English

## ซ

|  |  |  |
|---|---|---|
| เซ็นชื่อ | sen chûu | to sign (form, cheque, etc.) |
| ซิการ์ | si-gâa | cigar |
| ซีดี | sii-dii | CD |
| ซุปเปอร์มาร์เก็ต | súp-bpôr-maa-gét | supermarket |
| แซลมอน | saen-mô:n | salmon |
| ซ่อม | sô:m | fix |
| เซฟ | safe | safe |
| ซองจดหมาย | song-jòt-mǎai | envelope |
| ญาติ | yâat | relative |
| ตำแหน่ง | tàa-ná | position, status |
| เฒ่า | tâo | very old person |
| เณร | neen | Buddhist novice |

## ด

|  |  |  |
|---|---|---|
| ดูแล | duu-lae | to look after someone |
| ดึง | dung | to pull |
| เด็กผู้ชาย | dèk pôu chaai | boy |
| ดาว | daao | star |
| ด้าย | dâai | thread |
| ดัง | dang | loud |
| ดี | dii | well |
| ได้กลิ่น | dâai glìn | to smell |
| ดีที่สุด | dii-tîi-sùt | the best |
| โดยรถไฟ | duoy rót-fai | by train |
| โดยทันที | duoy tan-tii | immediately |
| โดยรถบัส | duoy rót-bus | by bus |
| ด้วย | dôoy | with |
| ด้วยกัน | dôoy-gan | together |
| ด่านศุลกากร | dàan sǔn-lá-gaa-gorn | customs control |

| Thai | | English |
|---|---|---|
| ดำน้ำ | dam náam | to dive |
| ดี | dii | good |
| ดื่ม | dùum | drink |
| เด็ก | dèk | child |
| เด็กนักเรียน | dèk nák rian | student |
| เดิน | dern | to walk |
| เดือน | duan | month |
| ตุลาคม | dtu-la-kom | October |
| ตั๋วชั้นสอง | dtŭa chán sŏng | a second-class ticket |
| ตั๋วไปกลับ | dtŭa bpai glàb | return (ticket) |
| ต่อกิโลเมตร | dtòr gi-loo-met | per kilometre |
| ต้นไม้ | dtôn-máai | tree |
| ตกลง | dtòk-long | OK |
| ใต้ | dtâi | south |
| เตียงคู่ | dtiang kûu | double bed |
| ตอนเย็น | dtorn yen | evening |
| ตู้โทรศัพท์ | dtûu too-rá-sàp | telephone box |
| ตกลงไหม | dtòk-long mái | all right (OK)? |

| Thai | | English |
|---|---|---|
| ตรงไปตี้ | dtrong bpai tii | straight on |
| ตลอดไป | dta-lòrd bpai | always |
| ตลอดไป | dta-lòrd bpai | forever |
| ต่อคน | dtòr kon | per person |
| ต้องห้าม | dtông hâam | forbidden |
| ต่อชั่วโมง | dtòr chûamoong | per hour |
| ตอนเช้า | dtorn cháo | morning |
| ตอบ | dtòrb | to answer |
| ต่อรอง | dtòr rorg | bargain |
| ตะกร้า | dtà-grâa | basket |
| ตะวันตก | dtà wan dtòk | west |
| ตัด | dtàt | cut |
| ตัดผม | dtàt-pŏm | haircut |
| ตัน | dtan | blocked |
| ตัวแทน | dtua taen | agent |
| ตั๋วไปกลับ | dtŭa bpai glàb | return ticket |
| ตั๋วเที่ยวเดียว | dtŭa tîao diao | single ticket |
| ตา | dtaa | eye |
| ตาบอด | dtaa-bòrt | blind (person) |
| ตาม | dtaam | to follow |

Thai – English

# Thai – English

| Thai | | English |
|---|---|---|
| ดินสอดมป์ | dtìd sà-dtaem | to put a stamp on (an envelope) |
| ติดต่อสอบถาม | dtìd-dtòr sòrb-tǎam | enquiry desk |
| ติดต่อสอบถาม | dtìd-dtòr sòrb-tǎam | information office |
| น่าตื่นเต้น | nâa-dtùun-dtên | exciting |
| ตุ๊กตา | dtúk-gà-dtaa | doll |
| ตู้เย็น | dtûu-yen | fridge |
| ตู้ไปรษณีย์ | dtûu prai-sa-nii | postbox |
| ตก | dtòk | to fall |
| ตกปลา | dtòk bplaa | to fish |
| ต้ม | dtôm | boiled (food) |
| ตรง | dtrong | direct |
| ตลาดนัด | dtà-làat-nát | bazaar, an open market |
| ต่อ | dtòr | per |
| ต่อ | dtòr | connection (train, plane) |
| ต่อไป | dtòr bpai | next |

| Thai | | English |
|---|---|---|
| ต้องการ | dtông-gaan | to need |
| ต้องการ | dtông-gaan | to want |
| ตอนนี้ | dton nii | now |
| ต่อย | dtòi | sting |
| ต่อว่า | dtòr-wâa | complain |
| ตะปู | dtà-bpuu | nail (metal) |
| ตะวันออก | dtà-wan-òrk | east |
| ตั๋ว | dtǔa | ticket |
| ตัวเลข | dtua lêek | number |
| ตัวต่อ | dtua dtòr | wasp |
| ตารางเวลา | dtaa-raang wee-laa | timetable |
| ตารางการบิน | dtaa-raang-gaan bin | flight |
| ตำรวจ | dtam-rùat | police |
| ตำรวจดับเพลิง | dtam-rùat dàp-plurng | firemen |
| ติดหนี้ | dtìd-nii | to owe |
| ตื่น | dtùun | to wake up |
| ตู้เสื้อผ้า | dtûu-sûa-pâa | wardrobe |

| เต็ม | dtem | full |
|---|---|---|
| แตงกวา | dtaeng-gwaa | cucumber |
| โต๊ะ | dtó | table |
| โต๊ะสำหรับเด็ก | dtó:sǎm-ràp dèk | high chair |
| เต็นท์ | dtén | tent |
| เตาอบ | dtao-òp | oven |
| เติม | dturm | to fill (up) |
| เตียงคู่ | dtiang kûu | double bed |
| เตียงเดี่ยวคู่ | dtiang diao kûu | twin beds |
| เตียง | dtiang | bed |
| เต้นรำ | dtên-ram | to dance |
| โต้คลื่น | dtôo klûun | surfing |
| โต๊ะเก็บเงิน | dtó gèb ngum | cash desk |

| ถั่วลิสง | tùa-lí-sŏng | peanuts |
|---|---|---|
| ถังน้ำ | tǎng náam | bucket |
| ถนน | tà-nǒn | street |
| ถั่ว | tùa | nuts |

## ท

| ทุกทุก | túk túk | every |
|---|---|---|
| ที่โกนหนวด | tîi goon nùat | shaver |
| ที่นั่ง | tîi nâng | seat, chair (on bus, train, etc.) |
| ที่เปิดไวน์ | tîi bpùrd wine | corkscrew |
| ทิ้ง | tíng | left |
| ทำ | tam | to make |
| ทั้งหมด | táng-mòt | whole |
| ท้องฟ้า | tó:ng fáa | sky |
| ท่องเที่ยว | tô:ng-tîao | to travel |
| น้ำท่วม | náam-tûam | flood |
| ทราย | saai | sand |
| เทนนิส | ten-nís | tennis |
| เทป | téep | tape |
| เท่าไร? | tâo-rài? | how much? |
| เท่านั้น | tâo nán | only |
| เที่ยงวัน | tîang-wan | midday |
| ทดแทน | tót-taen | to compensate, to replace |

## Thai - English

# Thai – English

|  |  |  |
|---|---|---|
| หมวย | tá-naai | lawyer |
| ทอง | torng | gold |
| ท้อง | tórng | pregnant |
| ท้อง | tórng | stomach |
| ทอด | tôrt | fried (food) |
| ท่อน้ำ | tôr náam | drain (etc.) |
| ทั้งหมด | táng-mòt | all |
| ท่าเรือ | tâa ruua | port (harbour) |
| ทารก | taa-rók | baby |
| ทาง | taang | way |
| ทางข้าม | taang-kâam | pedestrian crossing |
| ทางด่วน | taang duan | motorway |
| ทางด่วน | taang duan | toll (on motorway) |
| ทางออก | taang òrk | way out |
| ทางเข้า | taang kâo | entrance |
| ทางหนีไฟ | taang nǐi fai | fire exit |
| ทางออก | taang òrk | exit |
| ทางออกฉุกเฉิม | taang òrk chùk-chǔm | emergency exit |
| ทำให้แห้ง | tam-hâi-hâeng | to dry |
| ทำการล็อค | tam gaan lock | to lock |
| ทำความสะอาด | tam kwaam sà-àat | to clean |
| ทำงาน | tam ngaan | to work |
| ทำด้วยมือ | tam dûay muu | hand-made |
| ทำอาหาร | tam aa-hǎan | to cook |
| ทำไม | tam-mai | why |
| ทิชชู่ | tít-chûu | tissues |
| ทิป | tip | tip (to waiter, etc.) |
| ที่ | tîi | at |
| ที่เขี่ยบุหรี่ | tîi kìa burìi | ashtray |
| ที่เปิดกระป๋อง | tîi bpèrt grà-bpǒng | can-opener |
| ที่แปรงผม | tîi bpraeng pǒm | hairbrush |
| ที่โชว์สินค้า | tîi show sin-káa | boots |
| ที่ไหน | tîi nǎi | where? |
| ที่กรอง | tîi grorng | filter |
| ที่กันแสง | tîi-gan-sǎeng | blinds (on window) |
| ที่ขายตั๋ว | tîi kǎai dtǔa | ticket office |

|  |  |  |
| --- | --- | --- |
| ที่ติดต่อสัมภาระขาหาย | tîi dtìt-dtòr săm-paa-rá hăai | left-luggage office |
| ที่ทำการไปรษณีย์ | tîi tam gaan prai-sa-nii | post office |
| ที่หวีผม | tîi wǐi pŏm | hairbrush |
| ที่นั่งเด็ก | tîi nâng dèk | car seat (for child) |
| ที่นั่น | tîi nân | there |
| ที่นี่ | tîi nîi | here |
| ที่ราบ | tîi-râap | plain |
| ที่ล้างรถ | tîi láang rót | car wash |
| ที่อยู่ | tîi yùu | address |
| ทุกทุกคน | túk túk kon | everyone |
| ทุกทุกปี | túk túk bpii | every year |
| ทุกวัน | túk wan | every day |
| ที่เป่าผม | tîi pào pŏm | hair dryer |
| ที่เปิดขวด | tîi bpùrd kùat | bottle-opener |
| ที่จอดรถ | tîi jòrd rót | car park |
| ที่บังแดด | tîi-bang-dàet | sunshade |
| ทีม | tim | team (football, etc.) |
| ที่รับกระเป๋าเดินทาง | tîi ráb grà-bpăo dum taang | baggage reclaim |
| ทุกทุกวัน | túk túk wan | every day |
| ต่างประเทศ | too dtaang bpra-têet | international |
| โทร | têet | call |
| โทรทัศน์ | too-rá-tát | television |
| โทรศัพท์ | too-rá-sàp | phone |
| โทรหา | too-hăa | to call (on phone) |
| ทะเล | tà-lee | sea |
| ทะเลสาบ | tà-lee sàap | lake |
| ทัวร์ | tuaa | tour |
| ทัวร์นำเที่ยว | tuaa nam tîao | guided tour |
| แท็กซี่ | táek-sîi | taxi |
| มิเตอร์แท็กซี่ | mí-dtur-tàek-sîi | meter (taxi) |
| เทปเพลง | têep-pleeng | tape (cassette) |
| เที่ยงคืน | tîang kuun | midnight |
| เทียน | tian | candle |
| แท้ | táe | genuine |
| โทร | too | to telephone |
| โทรศัพท์ | too-rá-sàp | telephone |

# Thai – English

# Thai – English

| Thai | | English |
|---|---|---|
| เทา | táao | foot |
| เธอ | tur | she |
| ธรรมดา | tam-mà-daa | simple |
| ธันวาคม | tam-waa-kom | December |
| ธาตุเหล็ก | tâat lèk | iron (mineral) |
| เตารีด | dtao-rít | iron |
| **น** | | |
| นมสด | nom sòt | fresh milk |
| นอน | nom | to sleep |
| นักหนังสือพิมพ์ | nák-nǎng-sǔu-pim | journalist |
| นั่น | nán | that |
| น่าเกลียด | nâa-glìat | ugly |
| นาที | naa-tii | minute |
| นาน | naan | long |
| นามสกุล | naam-sà-gun | surname |
| นำ | nam | bring |
| น้ำ | náam | water |
| น้ำแกง | náam-gaeng | mineral water |
| น้ำแอปเปิล | náam apple | apple juice |
| น้ำกลั่น | náam glàn | distilled water |
| น้ำจิ้ม | náam jîm | sauce |
| น้ำดื่ม | náam dùum | drinking water |
| น้ำตก | náam dtòk | waterfall |
| น้ำตาล | náam dtaan | sugar |
| น้ำตาลเทียม | náam dtaan tiam | sweetener |
| น้ำผึ้ง | náam-pûng | honey |
| น้ำมะเขือเทศ | náam má-kǔa-têet | tomato juice |
| น้ำมัน | náam man | oil |
| น้ำมันรถ | náam man rót | petrol |
| น้ำสะอาด | náam sà-àat | fresh water |
| น้ำหนัก | náam nàk | weight |
| น้ำหนึ่งแก้ว | náam nùng gâew | a glass of water |
| น้ำหอม | náam hǒm | perfume |
| น้ำหนึ่งขวด | náam nùng kùat | a bottle of water |
| น้ำส้ม | náam sôm | orange juice |
| น้ำยาทาเล็บ | náam-yaa-taa-lép | nail polish |

| Thai | | English |
|---|---|---|
| น้ำมันมะกอก | náam man mà-gòok | olive oil |
| น้ำผลไม้ | náam pónla-máai | fruit juice |
| น้ำชา | náam-chaa | tea |
| น้ำแข็ง | náam kǎeng | ice |
| น้ำเย็นเปล่า | náam kǎeng bplàao | iced water |
| น้ำแร่ | náam rǣ | mineral water |
| น้ำมะเขือเทศ | náam-má-kǔa-têet | tomato juice |
| น้ำมะนาว | náam ma-naow | lemonade |
| น้ำยาล้างเล็บ | náam-yaa-láang lép | nail polish remover |
| น้ำยาซักผ้า | náam yaa sák pâa | washing powder |
| นาฬิกา | naa-li-gaa | clock |
| นาฬิกาปลุก | naa-li-gaa-bplùk | alarm clock |
| น่ารัก | nâa-rák | lovely |
| นั่ง | nâng | sit |
| น้องสาว | nó:ng sǎao | younger sister |
| นก | nók | bird |

| Thai | | English |
|---|---|---|
| นมผง | nom-pǒng | powdered milk |
| นักศิลปะ | nák sín-lá-bpà | artist |
| หนัง | nǎng | cinema |
| หนังสือ | nǎng-sǔu | book |
| หน้าร้อน | nâa rórm | summer |
| หนาว | nǎao | cold |
| หนึ่งโหล | nùng-lǒo | dozen |
| นิ่ง | níng | still (still water) |
| นิดหน่อย | níd-nòi | a little |
| นิดหน่อย | níd-nòi a little | a little |
| นิ่ม | nîm | bit |
| | | soft |
| นิวซีแลนด์ | niu-sii-laen | New Zealand |
| นี่ | nîi | this |
| นักท่องเที่ยว | nák tò:ng-tîao | tourist |
| นมพร่องมันเนย | nom pro:ng man | skimmed milk |
| นี้ | neei | |
| นม | nom | milk |
| เนื้อวัว | núa-wua | beef |
| แนะนำ | náe-nam | to recommend |

## Thai – English

|  |  |  |
|---|---|---|
| หาฬิกาข้อมือ | naa-li-gaa kôr muu | watch (wrist) |
| เนื้อลูกวัว | núa lôuk wua | veal |
| น่ารัก | nâa-rák | pretty |
| น้ำผลไม้ | náam-pónla-máai | fruit juice |
| น้ำผึ้งพระจันทร์ | náam pûng prá-jan | honeymoon |
| นิทรรศการ | ni-tát-sà-gaan | exhibition |
| บวม | buam | swollen (finger, ankle, etc.) |
| บริติช | bri-tish | British |
| บริการ | bo-ri-gaan | service |
| ใบเสร็จ | bai-sèt | receipt |
| โบสถ์ | bòot | church |
| แบน | baen | flat |
| แบตเตอรี่รถ | bàet-dtur-rî-rót | battery (for car) |
| ถ่านไฟฉาย | tàan-fai-cháai | battery (for torch, camera) |
| ใบขับขี่ | bai-kàp-kìi | driving licence |

|  |  |  |
|---|---|---|
| เบนซินไร้สารตะกั่ว | ben-sin rái sǎan dta-gùa | unleaded petrol |
| เบียร์ | bia | beer |
| เบียร์หนึ่งขวด | bia nùng kùat | a bottle of beer |
| เบียร์อีกขวด | bia lìk kùat | another beer |
| บน | bon | on |
| บน/ด้านขวา | bon/dâan kwǎa | on/to the right |
| บรั่นดี | | brandy |
| บริเวณกางเต็นท์ | bo-ri-ween kâai sàk-rít | camp site |
| บริการซักรีด | bo-ri-gaan sàk-rít | laundry service |
| บริษัท | bo-ri-sàt | company (business) |
| บริษัทท่องเที่ยว | bo-ri-sàt tông-tîao | travel agent |
| บ่อย | bòi | often |
| บัตรโทรศัพท์ | bàt too-rá-sàp | phonecard |
| บัตรผ่านประตู | bàt pàan bpra-dtuu | boarding card |
| บันได | ban-dai | stairs |

| บางเวลา | baang wee-laa | sometimes |
|---|---|---|
| บางไหม | baang mái | any |
| บางคน | baang kon | someone |
| บางอย่าง | baang yàang | something |
| บาง | baang | some |
| บาดเจ็บ | bàat jèb | injured |
| บ้าน | bâan | home, house |
| บ้านเช่า | bâan châo | guest-house |
| บ่าย | bàai | afternoon |
| บุคคล | bùk-kon | person |
| บุหรี่ | bù-rìi | cigarettes |
| บริเวณค่าย<br>อยู่ไหน | bo-ri-ween kâai<br>yùu nái | where is the<br>camp site? |
| บัตรประจำตัว | bàt bpra-jam-<br>dtua | identification<br>card |
| บ่ายนี้ | bàai níi | this afternoon |
| บ่ายพรุ่งนี้ | bàai prûng níi | tomorrow<br>afternoon |
| บาร์ | bar | bar |
| บินตรง | bin drong | direct flight |

| บิสกิต | biscuit | biscuits |
|---|---|---|
| บุหรี่หนึ่งซอง | bù-rìi nùng so:ng | a packet of<br>cigarettes |
| ใบรับรอง | bai-ráp-rorng | certificate |
| ใบส่งของ | bai-sòng-ko:ng | invoice |
| ใบเก็บเงิน | bai-gèb ngum | bill |
| ใบราคา | bai raa-kaa | price list |
| ใบสั่งยา | bai- sàng yaa | prescription |
| ใบสาระแหน่ | bai-sa-rà-nàe | mints |
| ใบสำเนา | bai-sàm-nao | photocopy |
| เบิกเงิน | bùrg ngum | to cash |
| เบื่อ | bùa | bored (to feel) |
| ปิกนิก | bpic-nic | picnic |
| ปาก | bpàak | mouth |
| ป่วย | bpùai | ill |
| ฉันป่วย | chan bpùai | I am ill |
| ปลาหมึกยัก | bplaa-mùk-yák | octopus |
| ปลาสด | bplaa-sòt | fresh fish |
| ปลอดภัย | bplòrt pai | safe |

## Thai – English

# Thai – English

| | | |
|---|---|---|
| ไปที่สถานี | bpai ti sà-tǎa-nii | to the station |
| เป็นไปได้ | bpen bpai dâai | possible |
| เป็นไปไม่ได้ | bpen bpai mâi dâai | impossible |
| เปิด | bpùrd | to switch on |
| ประตู | bpra-dtuu | door |
| ปวด | bpùat | ache |
| ป่า | bpàa | forest |
| โปรดปราน | bpròot-bpraan | favourite |
| ปลัก | bplák | plug (electric) |
| เป้ | bpêe | backpack |
| เปิด | bpùrd | to open |
| เปิด | bpùrd | to turn on |
| ปฐมพยาบาล | bpà-tǒm-pa-yaa-baan | first aid |
| ปกติ | bpòk-gà-dti | usually |
| ประเทศไอร์แลนด์ | bprà-têet-ai-laen | Ireland |
| ประเพณี | bprà-pee-nii | tradition |
| ประกัน | bprà-gan | insurance |
| การประชุม | gaan bprà-chum | conference |

| | | |
|---|---|---|
| ประมาณ | bprà-maan | about |
| ปรารถนา | bpràad-ta-nǎa | to prefer |
| ปราศจาก | bpràat-sa-jàak | without |
| | | see GRAMMAR |
| ปราสาท | bpra-sàat | castle |
| ปล้น | bplôn | burglary |
| ปลาซาร์ดีน | bplaa-saa-diin | sardines |
| ปลาทูน่า | bplaa-tuu-nâa | tuna |
| ปลาหมึกตัวเล็ก | bplaa mùk dtua lék | squid |
| ปวดฟัน | bpùat-fan | toothache |
| ปวดหัว | bpùat hǔa | headache |
| ปั๊มน้ำมัน | bpâm náam man | petrol station |
| ปากกา | bpàak-gaa | pen |
| ป้ายรถเมล์ | bpâai rót-mee | bus stop |
| ปาร์ตี้ | bpaa-dtîi | party (celebration) |
| ปิ้ง | bping | toast |
| ปิงปอง | bping-bpo:ng | table tennis |
| ปิด | bpìd | shut |
| ปิด | bpìd | to switch off |

| | | |
|---|---|---|
| ปิด | bpìd | to turn off (radio, light) |
| ปิด | bpìd | to close |
| ปิด | bpìd | closed |
| ปี | bpii | year |
| ปีนี้ | bpii níi | this year |
| ปีใหม่ | bpii mài | New Year |
| ปีน | bpiin | climbing |
| ประเทศออสเตรเลีย | bprà-têet-òt-sa-dtree-lia | Australia |
| ประเทศอิตาลี | bprà-têeti-dtaa-lii | Italy |
| ประจำวัน | bpra jam wan | daily |
| ประจำสัปดาห์ | bpra jam sàp-daa | weekly |
| ปลา | bplaa | fish |
| ปวดหัว | bpùat hŭa | headache |
| ป่วย | bpùai | ill |
| ปู่ | bpùu | grandfather (paternal) |
| เปล | bplee | cot |

| | | |
|---|---|---|
| เปลี่ยน | bplìan | to change (money) |
| เปลือกหอย | bplùak-hŏi | shell |
| เปียก | bpìak | wet |
| แปล | bplae | to translate |
| แป้ง | bpâeng | flour |
| ไปรษณียบัตร | bprai-sa-nii-ya-bàt | postcard |
| ผู้สูงอายุ | pôu sŭung-aa-yú | senior citizen |
| ผ้าเช็ดมือ | pâa chét muu | hand towel |
| ผลัก | plàk | to push |
| แผ่นไม้ | pàen mái | wood (substance) |
| แผนที่ | pàen-tîi | map |
| แผ่นดินไหว | pàen-din-wǎi | earthquake |
| ผิวไหม้แดด | piu mâi dàet | sunburn |
| ผงซักฟอก | pŏng-sák-fôk | detergent |
| ผลไม้ | pŏnla-máai | fruit |
| ผลไม้สด | pŏnla-máai sòt | fresh fruit |
| ผอม | pŏrm | thin |

Thai – English

# Thai – English

|  |  |  |
|---|---|---|
| ผักใบเขียว | pàk-bai-kĭao | green leaves (vegetable) |
| ผ้าเช็ดปาก | pâa chét bpàak | napkin |
| ผ่านไปแล้ว | pàan bpai láew | ago |
| ผ้าปูที่เตียง | pâa-bpuu-dtiang | sheet (for bed) |
| ผ้าปูที่นอน | pâa-bpuu-tîi-nom | bedclothes |
| ผ้าลินิน | pâa linin | linen |
| ผ้าห่ม | pâa-hòm | blanket |
| ผิด | pìd | wrong |
| ผิว | pĭu | skin |
| ผื่น | pùun | rash (skin) |
| ผู้โดยสาร | pûu duoy sàan | passenger |
| ผู้ใหญ่ | pûu yài | adult |
| ผู้ชาย | pûu chaai | man |
| ผู้มาเยี่ยม | pûu maa yîam | visitor |
| ผู้หญิง | pûu-yĭng | woman |
| เผ็ด | pèt | spicy |
| แผลพุพอง | plăe pú-po:ng | blister |
| ผม | pŏm | hair |
| ผัก | pàk | vegetable |

|  |  |  |
|---|---|---|
| ผักสด | pàk sòt | fresh vegetables |
| ผ้าเช็ดตัว | pâa chét dtua | towel |
| ผ้าพันแผล | pâa-pan-plăe | bandage |
| ผึ้ง | pûng | bee |
| ผู้จัดการ | pûu-jàt-gaan | manager |
| ผู้นำทัวร์ | pûu nam tuaa | a guide |
| ผู้ปกครอง | pûu bpòk-krorng | parents |
| ฝาก | fàak | deposit |
| ฝน | fŏn | rain |
| ฝักบัว | fàk bua | shower (bath) |
| ฝั่งทะเล | fang-tá-lee | coast |
| พ | | |
| พูด | pûud | to say |
| พุดดิ้ง | pùd-dîng | pudding |
| พิเศษ | pí-sèet | special |
| พักผ่อน | pák pòn | to rest |
| พ่อ | pôr | father |
| พวกเขา | pûag-kăo | they |
| พลาสติก | pláas-tìk | plastic |

| พฤศจิกายน | prʉ́t-sà-ji-gaa-yon | November | | พนักงานต้อนรับ | pa-nôk-ngaan dtô:n-ráp | receptionist |
| พรุ่งนี้ตอนเช้า | prûng níi dtorn | tomorrow | | พยากรณ์อากาศ | pa-yaa-gorn aa-gàat | weather forecast |
| พร้อม | cháo | morning | | พยาบาล | pa-yaa-baan | nurse |
| พรม | próhm | ready | | พระจันทร์ | prá-jan | moon |
| พรม | prom | rug; carpet | | พระอาทิตย์ | prá-aa-tít | sun |
| หนังงานขายพรม | pa-nák-ngaan kǎai | shop assistant | | พริกไทย | prík-tai | pepper (spice) |
| แพนเค้ก | paen-cake | pancake | | พรุ่งนี้ | prûng níi | tomorrow |
| เพนนิซิลิน | pen-nî-si-lin | penicillin | | พรุ่งนี้เย็น | prûng níi yen | evening |
| แพง | paeng | expensive | | พฤษภาคม | prʉ́t-sa-paa-kom | May |
| เพิ่ม | pûm | extra | | พลาด | plâad | miss (plane, train, etc.) |
| เพื่อน | pûan | friend | | พอดี | por-dii | fit |
| พ่อตาของฉัน | pôr dtaa kö:ng chan | my father-in-law | | พ่อตา | pôr dtaa | father-in-law |
| เพียงพอ | piang-por | enough | | พัก | pák | to stay |
| พจนานุกรม | pót-jà-naa-nú-grom | dictionary | | พาย | paai | pie |
| พนักงานเสิร์ฟ | pa-nák-ngaan sùrp | waiter/waitress | | พายุ | paa-yú | storm |
| พนักงานขาย | pa-nák-ngaan kǎai salesperson | | | พาสต้า | pas-dtâa | pasta |
| | | | | พิษ | pit | poisonous |

**Thai – English**

# Thai - English

|  |  |  |
|---|---|---|
| พี่ชาย | pîi-chaai | brother |
| พูด | pûud | to speak |
| ฟองน้ำ | fong náam | sponge (for cleaning) |
| ไฟลวกมือฉัน | fai-lûak-muu-chan | I've burned my hand |
| ไฟแช็ก | fai-shék | lighter (cigarette) |
| แฟน | faen | boyfriend |
| แฟลต | flat | flat (apartment) |
| ฟิล์ม | film | film |
| ฟ้า | fáa | blue |
| ฟันปลอม | fan-bplom | dentures |
| ฟัน | fan | teeth |
| เฟอร์นิเจอร์ | fur-ni-jùr | furniture |
| การเพิ่มค่าภาษี | paa-sí-muun-la-kâa-pôrm | VAT |
| ภาพวาด | pâap-wâad | painting (picture) |
| ภรรยา | panrayaa | wife |

|  |  |  |
|---|---|---|
| ภูมิแพ้ | puum-páe | allergy |
| ภูเขา | puu-kǎo | mountain |
| ภาพ | pâap | picture (on wall) |
| มีประโยชน์ | mii-bprà-yòot | useful |
| มีดโกน | mîit-goon | razor |
| มิถุนายน | mí-tù-naa-yon | June |
| มากไป | mâak bpai | too much |
| มาก | mâak | very |
| มันเสีย | man sia | this is off (milk, food) |
| ไม่มีอะไร | mâi mii a-rai | nothing |
| ไม้ขีด | máai-kìit | matches (light) |
| ไม่ | mâi | no |
| ไม่เคย | mâi keei | never |
| แม่ | mâe | mother |
| แมลง | ma-laeng | insect |
| แมว | maew | cat |
| มาถึง | maa tǔng | to come (arrive) |
| มัน | man | greasy |

| Thai | | English |
|---|---|---|
| มด | mót | ants |
| มหาวิทยาลัย | mà-hăa-wít-ta-yaa-lai | university |
| มองหา | mong-hăa | to look for |
| มะเขือเทศ | mà-kŭa-têet | tomato |
| มะกอก | mà-gòk | olives |
| มะพร้าว | mà-práao | coconut |
| มังสวิรัติ | mang-sà-wí-rát | vegetarian |
| มัน | man | it |
| มันดีมาก | man dii mâak | it's very nice |
| มันติด | man dtìt | it's stuck |
| ติด | dtìt | stuck |
| มันฝรั่งทอด | man-fa-ràng-tôrt | fried potatoes |
| มันฝรั่งบด | man-fa-ràng-bòd | mashed potato |
| มันปิดหรือ | man bpìd rŭu | is it closed? |
| เปล่า | bplàao | (building, etc.) |
| มันฝรั่ง | man-fa-ràng | potato |
| มันฝรั่งทอดกรอบ | maan fa-ràng tôrt kròrp | potato chips |
| มันอายุกี่ปี | man aa-yú gìi bpii? | how old is it? |
| ม้า | máa | horse |
| มาก | mâak | a lot |
| มากมาก | mâak mâak | lot |
| มาก | mâak | more |
| มาถึง | maa tŭng | to arrive |
| มัสตาร์ด | mát-sa-tàad | mustard |
| มีโทรศัพท์มา | mii too-rá-sàp maa | telephone call |
| มีด | mîit | knife |
| มีนาคม | mii-naa-kom | March |
| มีสระน้ำไหม | mii sà-nàam mái? | Is there a pool? |
| มืด | mûud | dark |
| มือ | muu | hand |
| มุ้ง | múng | mosquito net |
| มูลค่า | muun-la-kâa | value |
| มีตำหนิ | mii dtam-ni | fault (defect) |
| แม่ยาย | mâe-yaai | mother-in-law |
| ไม่สะดวก | mâi sà-dùak | inconvenient |
| มีชื่อเสียง | mii chûu-siang | famous |
| เมื่อคืน | mûa kuun | last night |

Thai – English

|  |  |  |
|---|---|---|
| เมื่อย | mûai | tired, stiff |
| เมษายน | mee-săa-yon | April |
| ยุ่ง | yûng | busy |
| ยุโรป | yú-rôop | Europe |
| ยานอนหลับ | yaa-nom-làp | sleeping pill |
| ยาก | yâak | difficult |
| ยา | yaa | pill |
| เยี่ยม | yîam | to visit |
| ยกเลิก | yók-lôrk | cancel |
| ยา | yâa | grandmother (paternal) |
| ยาแก้ปวด | yaa-gâe-bpùat | painkiller |
| ยาก | yâak | hard (tough) |
| ยาคุมกำเนิด | yaa-kum-gam-nùrt | contraceptive pill |
| ยาฆ่าเชื้อโรค | yaa-kâa-chúa-rôok | disinfectant |
| ย่าง | yâang | grilled |
| ยาสีฟัน | yaa-sĭi-fan | toothpaste |

|  |  |  |
|---|---|---|
| ยินดีต้อนรับ | yindii dtôːn ráp! | welcome! |
| ยิ้ม | yim | smile |
| ยุง | yung | mosquitoes |
| ยอดเยี่ยม | yôrt-yîam | excellent |
| ยางยืด | yaang-yúud | elastic band |
| แยกกัน | yâek gan | separately |
| ๆ | | |
| รายการไวน์ | raai-gaan wine | wine list |
| ร้านขายของ | ráan kăai kǒːng | souvenir shop |
| ฝาก | fâak | |
| ราชินี | raa-chi-nii | queen |
| ระเบียบข้อบังคับ | rá-biap kôr bang-kàp | regulations |
| รองเท้าแตะ | romg-táao-dtàe | sandals |
| รองเท้า | romg-táao | shoes |
| รถเข็น | rót kén | wheelchair |
| รถเข็น | rót-kén | pushchair |
| โรงเรียน | roong-nan | school |
| เร็ว | reo | fast |

| | | |
|---|---|---|
| เรา | rao | we |
| เรือ | ruua | ship |
| เรือเล็ก | ruua lék | dinghy |
| รถเก๋ง | rót | car |
| รถไฟ | rót fai | train |
| รถไฟเที่ยวแรก | rót fai tîao râek | the first train |
| รถไฟใต้ดิน | rót fai dtâi din | underground (metro) |
| รถตู้ | rót dtûu | van |
| รถบรรทุก | rót-ban-túk | truck |
| รถบัส | rót-bus | bus |
| รถบัสเที่ยวแรก | rót-bus tîao râek | the first bus |
| รวมทั้งหมด | ruam-táng-mót | total |
| รวย | ruai | rich (person) |
| รหัสโทรศัพท์ | ra-hàt too-rá-sàp | dialling code |
| รหัสไปรษณีย์ | ra-hàt prai-sa-nii | zip code |
| รอ | ror | to wait (for) |
| รองเท้าแตะ | ro:ng-táao dtæ̀ | slippers |
| ร้องไห้ | róng-hâai | to cry (weep) |
| ระบบเตือนภัย | ra-bòb-dtuan-pai | alarm system |

| | | |
|---|---|---|
| รัก | rák | to love |
| รับ | ráb | to accept |
| ราคา | raa-kaa | cost |
| ราคา | raa-kaa | price |
| ร้าน | ráan | shop |
| ร้านเค้ก | ráan-cake | cake shop |
| ร้านเพลง | ráan pleeng | music shop |
| ร้านขายของขวัญ | ráan kǎai kǒ:ng-kwǎn | gift shop |
| ร้านซักแห้ง | ráan sák hâeng | dry-cleaner's |
| ร้านสินค้าปลอดภาษี | ráan sin-káa bplòt paa-sǐi | duty-free shop |
| ร้านหนังสือ | ráan nǎng-sǐu | bookshop |
| รายการ | raai-gaan | menu |
| รู้ | rúu | to know |
| ระเบียง | rá-biang | terrace |
| โรคกลัวน้ำ | rôok-glua-náam | rabies |
| รู้สึก | rúu-sùk | feel |
| ร่ม | rôm | umbrella |
| เรือข้ามฟาก | ruua-kâam-fâak | ferry |

Thai – English

# Thai - English

| Thai | Phonetic | English |
|------|----------|---------|
| เรียมอยด | ruua yót | yacht |
| ลูกชาย | lûuk-chaai | son |
| ลอเลน | lór-lên | joke, to tease |
| ลมแรง | lom raeng | windy |
| เล็ก | lék | little (small) |
| ลิ้นชัก | lín-chák | drawer |
| ลายเซ็น | laai-sen | signature |
| ล่ามโซ่ | lâam-sôo | to chain |
| ล่าม | lâam | interpreter |
| ล้าง | láang | to wash |
| ล็อกเกอร์ | lock-gur | locker (for luggage) |
| ล็อก | lock | lock |
| ลงรถ | long rót | to get off (bus, etc.) |
| ลงจอด | long jòrt | landing |
| ลึก | lúk | deep |
| ล่าช้า | lâa-cháa | delay |
| ลิปสติก | lip-sa-dtick | lipstick |

| Thai | Phonetic | English |
|------|----------|---------|
| ลูกเกด | lûuk gèet | raisins |
| ลูกเทนนิส | lûuk ten-nís | tennis ball |
| ลูกบอล | lûuk-bo:n | ball |
| ลูกสาว | lûuk săao | daughter |
| เล็ก | lék | small |
| เล็กกว่า | lék gwàa | smaller |
| เล่น | lên | to play |
| เล่นสเก็ต | lên-sa-gèt | to skate |
| เลือด | lûat | blood |
| เลือดกรุ๊ป | lûat-group | blood group |
| เลือดออก | lûat òrk | to bleed |
| วัน | wan | day |
| วันเกิด | wan gùrt | birthday |
| วันเกิด | wan gùrt | date of birth |
| วันที่ | wan tîi | date (calendar) |
| วันนี้ | wan níi | today |
| วันหยุด | wan yùd | holiday |
| วันหยุด(ราชการ)ใน | wan yùd tûa bpai | public holiday |
| วันหลัง | wan lăng | later |

|  |  |  |
|---|---|---|
| วันจันทร์ | wan-jan | Monday |
| วันเสาร์ | wan-são | Saturday |
| วันพุธ | wan-pút | Wednesday |
| วันพฤหัสบดี | wan-pá-rú-hàt-sa-bo-dii | Thursday |
| วันอาทิตย์ | wan aa-tít | Sunday |
| วันอังคาร | wan ang-kaan | Tuesday |
| วัด | wát | measure |
| ไวน์แดง | wine-daeng | red wine |
| ไวน์ | wine | wine |
| เวรรอบดึก | ween-rôrb-dùk | night duty |
| เภสัชกร | pee-sàt-cha-gorn | chemist |
| วงจร | wong-jorn | a cycle |
| ว่าง | wâang | free (unoccupied) |
| ว่างเปล่า | wâang bplàao | empty |
| ว่างงาน | wâang ngaan | unemployed |
| ว่ายน้ำ | wâai-náam | to swim |
| วิทยุ | wít-ta-yú | radio |

|  |  |  |
|---|---|---|
| วินาที | vi-naa-tii | second |
| วีซ่า | vii-sâa | visa |
| วิตามิน | vi-dtaa-min | vitamin pills |
| วอลเลย์บอล | vol-lêe-bo:n | volleyball |
| ศุลกากร | sŭn-la-gaa-gorn | customs |
| ศูนย์กลาง | sŭun-glaang | central |
| ศาลากลาง | săa-laa-glaang | town hall |
| ศูนย์ | sŭun | zero |
| ศูนย์กลางเมือง | sŭun glaang muang | city centre |
| ศูนย์กลางเมือง | sŭun glaang muang | town centre |
| ศูนย์บริการนักท่องเที่ยว | sŭun bo-ri-gaan nák-tô:ng-tîao | tourist office |
| เศร้า | são | sad |
| เศษสตางค์ | sèet-sa-dtaang | change (loose coins) |

# Thai - English

| Thai | | English |
|---|---|---|
| ญ | | |
| ญุ้ง | sǔung | tall |
| สีสม | sǐi sôm | orange (colour) |
| สีแดง | sǐi daeng | red |
| สำหรับขาย | sǎm-ráp kǎai | for sale |
| สาย | sǎai | late |
| สามี | sǎa-mii | husband |
| สั้น | sân | short |
| สั่งอาหาร | sàng aa-hǎan | to order (food) |
| สะกด | sà-gòt | spell |
| สลัดมันฝรั่ง | sà-làd man-fa-ràng | potato salad |
| สลัด | sà-làd | salad |
| สถานีรถไฟ | sà-tǎa-nii rót fai | railway station |
| สถานีสูญกลาง | sa-tǎa-nii sǔun-glaang | central station |
| สถานกงสุล | sà-tǎan-gong-sǔn | consulate |
| โสด | sòod | single |
| เสื้อ | sûa | shirt |
| เสื้อกันฝน | sûa gan fǒn | raincoat |

| Thai | | English |
|---|---|---|
| เสื้อแจ็คเก็ต | sûa-jàek-gét | jacket |
| เสื้อกันหนาว | sûa-gan-nǎao | sweater |
| เสื้อหนัง | sûa nǎng | leather jacket |
| เสื้อชูชีพ | sûa-chuu-chîp | life jacket |
| เสื้อผ้า | sûa phâa | clothes |
| เสื้อยืด | sûa yûud | t-shirt |
| เสื้อคลุม | sûa klum | coat |
| สก็อตแลนด์ | sà-gò:t-laen | Scotland |
| สกีน้ำ | sà-gii ndam | water-skiing |
| ส่ง | sòng | to send |
| สงคราม | sòng-kraam | war |
| ส่งต่อ | sòng dtòr | forward(s) |
| สด | sòt | fresh |
| สเก็ต | sà-gèt | skates |
| สมุนไพร | sà-mún-prai | herbs |
| สลัดผลไม้ | sà-làd pòhla-máai | fruit salad |
| สวน | sǔan | park |
| สวย | sǔay | beautiful |
| สวัสดี | sà-wàd-dii | good day |
| สวิตช์ | sà-wìt | switch |

| Thai | | English |
|---|---|---|
| สมบูรณ์แบบ | sŏm-buun-bàep | perfect |
| สถานทูต | sa-tǎan tûut | embassy |
| สถานทูตอังกฤษ | sa-tǎantûut ang-grìt | British embassy |
| อังกฤษ | ang-grìt | British |
| สถานกงสุลอังกฤษ | sà-tǎan-gong-sǔn ang-grìt | consulate |
| กงสุล | sún ang-grìt | |
| สถานกงสุลอเมริกัน | sà-tǎan-gong-sǔn a-mee-ri-gaa | American consulate |
| อเมริกา | | |
| สถานทูตอเมริกา | sa-tǎan tûut a-mee-ri-gaa | American embassy |
| อเมริกา | | |
| สถานีตำรวจ | sà-tǎa-nii dtam-rùat | police station |
| สถานี | sà-tǎa-nii | station |
| สถานีรถเมล์อยู่ที่ไหน | sà-tǎa-nii kon sŏng yuu tîi nâi? | where is the bus station? |
| สถานีดับเพลิง | sà-tǎa-nii-dàp-plurng | fire brigade |
| สถานีรถเมล์ | sà-tǎa-nii kon sŏng | bus station |

| Thai | | English |
|---|---|---|
| สนใจ | sŏn-jai | to be interested in |
| สนามเทนนิส | sà-nǎam ten-nís | tennis court |
| สนามกีฬา | sà-nǎam gii-laa | stadium |
| สนามบิน | sà-nǎam-bin | airport |
| สบาย | sà-baai | comfortable |
| สบู่ | sà-bùu | soap |
| ส้ม | sôm | orange |
| สมุดเช็ค | sà-mùt chéck | cheque book |
| สระน้ำ | sà-nǎam | pool |
| สระว่ายน้ำ | sà-wâai nǎam | swimming-pool |
| สลัดมะเขือเทศ | sà-làd má-kŭa-têet | tomato salad |
| สวน | sǔan | garden |
| สวนบุคคล | sǔan bùk-kon | private |
| สวนลด | sǔan lód | discount |
| สวนสัตว์ | sǔan sàt | zoo |
| สวัสดี | sà-wàd-dii | hello |
| สัปดาห์ที่แล้ว | sàp-daa tîi láew | last week |
| สากล | sǎa-gon | international |

**Thai – English**

# Thai – English

|  |  |  |
|---|---|---|
| สำคัญ | sǎm-kan | important |
| สำหรับ | sǎm-ráp | for |
| สัญชาติ | sǎn-châat | nationality |
| สัญญาณ | sǎn-yaan | sign (road, notice, etc.) |
| สัญญาณไฟ | sǎn-yaan dtuan fai | fire alarm |
| สับ | sàp | chop (meat) |
| สัปดาห์ | sàp-daa | week |
| สัปดาห์หน้า | sàp-daa nâa | next week |
| สามีของฉัน | sǎa-mii kǒng chan | my husband |
| สามีภรรยา | sǎamii-panraya | couple (two people) |
| สำนักงาน | sǎm-nák-ngaan | office |
| สิงหาคม | sing-hǎa-kom | August |
| สี | sǐi | colour |
| สีน้ำตาล | sǐi-náam-dtaan | brown |
| สีม่วง | sǐi mûang | purple |
| สุเหร่า | sù-rào | mosque |
| สุกสุก | sùk sùk | well done (meat) |
| สุขสันต์วันเกิด | sùk-sǎn wan-gùrt | Happy Birthday! |
| สูง | sǔung | high |
| สูตรอาหาร | sùut aa-hǎan | recipe |
| สูท | sùut | suit (clothes) |
| สูบบุหรี่ | sùub bu-rìi | to smoke |
| เสร็จ | sèt | finish |
| สูงชัน | sǔung-chan | steep |
| สกปรก | sòk-gà-bpròk | dirty |
| สมุดโทรศัพท์ | sà-mùt too-rá-sàp | directory (telephone) |
| สำหรับฉัน | sǎm-ráp chan | for me |
| เสียหาย | sia hǎai | damage |
| แสดง | sa-daeng | show |
| แสตมป์ | sà-dtaem | stamp |
| หิว (น้ำ) | hiu (náam) | thirsty |
| หายใจ | hǎai-jai | to breathe |
| หัวใจ | hǔa-jai | heart |
| ห้องว่าง | hông wâang | vacancy (room) |
| ห้องครัว | hông krua | kitchen |

|  |  |  |
|---|---|---|
| ห้องขายตั๋ว | hôːng kǎai dtǔa | box office |
| ห้องเดี่ยว | hôːng diao | single room |
| หวี | wǐi | comb |
| หวัด | wàt | cold |
| หลังคา | lǎng-kaa | roof |
| หลอดไฟ | lòrd-fai | light bulb |
| หรือ | rǔu | or |
| หยุด | yùd | stop! |
| หยุด | yùd | quit |
| หนู | nǔu | rat |
| หนึ่ง | nùng | one |
| หนัง | nǎng | leather |
| ให้ | hâi | to let (allow) |
| หูหนวก | hǔu-nùak | deaf |
| หูเจ็บ | hǔu jèb | ear ache |
| หุ้นส่วน | hûn-sùan | partner (business) |
| หาย | hǎai | missing (thing) |
| ห้ามสูบบุหรี่ | hâam sùub-bu-rìi | non-smoking |
| ห้างสรรพสินค้า | hâang sàp-pa-sin-kâa | department store |

|  |  |  |
|---|---|---|
| หัวหอมใหญ่ | hǔa-hǒːm-yài | onion |
| หัวมุม | hǔa mum | corner |
| หอย | hǒi | shellfish |
| ห้องอาหาร | hôːng aa-hǎan | restaurant |
| ห้องน้ำสุภาพสตรี | hôːng náam sù-pâap-sà-dtrii | ladies' (toilet) |
| ห้องนั่งรอ | hôːng nâng ror | waiting room |
| ห้องทานอาหาร | hôːng taan aa-hǎan | dining room |
| ห้องคู่ | hôːng kûu | double room |
| ห้องแสดงศิลปะ | hôːng sa-daeng sǐn-lá-bpà | gallery (art) |
| ห้องเปลี่ยนเสื้อผ้า | hôːng bplian sûa-pâa | changing-room |
| ห้อง | hôːng | room |
| ห่อ | hòr | wrap |
| หลานสาว | lǎan-sǎao | niece |
| หลานชาย | lǎan-chaai | nephew |
| ภายหลัง | paai-lǎng | after |
| หลัง | lǎng | back (of body) |

# Thai – English

|  |  |  |
|---|---|---|
| หมายถึง | mǎai tǔng | mean |
| หมายเลขทะเบียน | mǎai lêk tà-bian | number plate |
| หมายเลขโทรศัพท์ | mǎai lêk too-rá-sàp | phone number |
| หมากฝรั่ง | màak-fà-ràng | chewing-gum |
| หมั้น | mân | engaged (to be married) |
| หม้อ | môr | pot (for cooking) |
| หมวก | mùak | hat |
| หนู | nǐu | mouse |
| หน้า | nâa | face |
| หนังสือพิมพ์ | nǎng-sǔu-pim | newspaper |
| หนังสือแนะนำ | nǎng-sǔu-nǽe-nam | guide/ guidebook |
| หนังสือเดินทาง | nǎng-sǔu dern taang | passport |
| หนัก | nàk | heavy |
| หน่วยกู้ภัย | nùai gûu pai | lifeguard |
| หนวด | nùat | moustache |

|  |  |  |
|---|---|---|
| หนวกหู | nùak hǔu | noisy |
| เหมือน | mǔan | same |
| หมดอายุ | mòt aa-yú | to expire |
| ใหญ่ | yài | big |
| หมอน | mǒn | pillow |
| หมอฟัน | mǒr fan | dentist |
| สมุดโทรศัพท์ | nǎng-sǔu too-rá-sàp | telephone directory |
| ห้องนอนเดี่ยว | hông-nom diao | single bedroom |
| หลอดไฟ | lòrt-fai | bulb (light) |
| หิว | hǐu | hungry |
| ฉันหิวข้าว | chan hǐu kâao | I'm hungry |
| อา/น้า/ป้า | aa | aunt (father's younger sister)/ |
|  | náa | (mother's younger sister)/ |
|  | bpâa | (parents' older sister) |
| อาหาร | aa-hǎan | food |

| | | | | | |
|---|---|---|---|---|---|
| อาหารหลัก | aa-hǎan-làk | main course (of meal) | ไอศกรีม | ai-sa-kriim | ice cream |
| อาหารเช้า | aa-hǎan cháao | breakfast | อก | òk | chest (of body) |
| อาหารเย็น | aa-hǎan yen | evening meal | อธิบาย | à-tí-baai | to explain |
| อาหารค่ำ | aa-hǎan kâm | dinner (evening meal) | อพาร์ตเมนต์ | a-pàat-mén | apartment |
| อาหารทารก | aa-hǎan taa-rók | baby food | อย่างเร็ว | yàang reo | quickly |
| อาหารสำเร็จรูป | aa-hǎan sǎm-rèt-rûub | delicatessen | อร่อย | aròy | tasty |
| อีกครั้ง | ìik kráng | again | อร่อย | aròy | delicious |
| อีสุกอีใส | i-sùk-i-sǎi | chickenpox | อ้วน | ûan | fat (person) |
| อื่น อื่น | ùun ùun | other | ไขมัน | kǎi-man | fat (food) |
| อิสลาม | it-sa-laam | Muslim | ออก | òrk | out |
| อ่างล้างหน้า | àang láang nâa | washbasin | ออกไป | òrk bpai | to go out |
| อ่างล้างจาน | àang láang jaan | sink | อักเสบ | àk-sèep | infection |
| อัตรา | àt-dtraa | rate | อักเสบ | àk-sèep | to become inflamed |
| ออกค่าย | òrk-kâai | to camp | อังกฤษ | ang-grìt | England |
| ออกเรือ | òrk ruua | sailing | อันไหน | an nǎi? | which one? |
| ออก | òrk | out | อันไหน | an nǎi? | which? |
| อนุญาต | à-nú-yâat | permit | อากาศดี | aa-gàat dii | fine (weather) |
| | | | อาบแดด | àap daèt | sunbathe |
| | | | อายุ | aa-yú | age |

Thai – English

# Thai - English

|  |  |  |
|---|---|---|
| อาศัย | aa-săi | to live |
| อาหาร | aa-hǎan | meal |
| อาหารกลางวัน | aa-hǎan glaang wan | lunch |
| อาหารทะเล | aa-hǎan tá-lee | seafood |
| อีเมล | e-mail | e-mail |
| อุโมงค์ | ù-moong | tunnel |
| อุ่น | ùn | warm |
| อ่าน | àan | to read |
| เอ็กซ์เรย์ | ék-sà-ree | x-ray |
| ไอริช | kon-ai-rish | Irish |
| อันตราย | an-dta-raai | dangerous |
| อุบัติเหตุ | ù-bàt-dti-hèet | accident |
| อุณหภูมิ | un-hà-puum | temperature |
| อเมริกา | a-mee-ri-gaa | America |
| องุ่น | a-ngùn | grapes |
| อย่างไร | yàang-rai? | how? |
| อย่างอื่น | yàang ùun | another |
| อยู่คนเดียว | yùu kon diao | alone |
| อะไร | a-rai? | what |

|  |  |  |
|---|---|---|
| อัตราแลกเปลี่ยน | àt-dtraa lâek bplian | exchange rate |
| แฮม | haem | ham |

# Further titles in Collins' phrasebook range
## Collins Gem Phrasebook

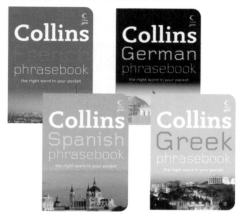

Also available as **Phrasebook CD Pack**
**Other titles in the series**

| | | |
|---|---|---|
| Arabic | Greek | Polish |
| Cantonese | Italian | Portuguese |
| Croatian | Japanese | Russian |
| Czech | Korean | Spanish |
| Dutch | Latin American | Thai |
| French | Spanish | Turkish |
| German | Mandarin | Vietnamese |